TRIPLE TESTED
FOR YOUR SUCCESS EVERY TIME

For more than 50 years, *The Australian Women's Weekly* Test Kitchen has been creating marvellous recipes that come with a guarantee of success. First, the recipes always work – just follow the instructions and you too will get the results you see in the photographs. Second, and perhaps more importantly, they are delicious – created by experienced home economists and chefs, all triple-tested and, thanks to their straightforward instructions, easy to make.

We enjoyed breaking from stir-frying traditions in this book. We stir-fried curries, spicy warm salads, pasta, Mediterranean-inspired dishes as well as delicious Asian recipes – all made quick and easy with a recipe style designed especially for speedy meal making. Prepare everything before you start to cook, then you can stir-fry meals in a matter of minutes. Perfect for today's busy lifestyles! But now, before you reach for a wok, read wok basics (page 4) and our stir-frying tips (page 6).

Pamela Clark

FOOD EDITOR

contents

wok basics

Although it looks simple, a wok is a highly efficient piece of cooking equipment. If you've never owned a wok before, here's an idea of what is available and how to get the best results from it.

choosing a wok Woks come in a variety of shapes, sizes and finishes, ranging from the traditional carbon steel wok to cast iron, stainless steel, non-stick and electric woks. The traditional, round-based woks are ideal for gas burners, while the flat-based woks are best used on electric stoves. You will notice, as you shop around, that woks also come with a variety of price tags, however an expensive one is not necessarily better than the inexpensive basic carbon steel wok, originally available from Asian supermarkets but now readily found in homeware stores, large supermarkets and hardware shops. For ease of handling, especially if you haven't used a wok before, it's best to choose one that has a long wooden handle, as metal handles can become very hot.

seasoning your wok Stainless steel and non-stick woks need nothing but a quick wash before their first use, but carbon steel and cast iron woks must be "seasoned" before they are used for the first time. Do not be tempted to skip this step – it will make all the difference to your stir-frying once your wok is properly seasoned, and if you take care of it, you will probably only need to do it once. First, wash the wok in hot soapy water to remove all traces of grease, then dry it thoroughly.

Place the wok on the stove over high heat; when hot, rub 1-2 tablespoons of cooking oil over the entire inside surface with absorbent paper. Wear oven gloves on both hands for this step as the oil and wok become very hot. Continue heating the wok for about 10-15 minutes, wiping from time to time with a ball of clean absorbent paper. This treatment will create a certain amount of smoke. Don't be alarmed – this is normal, because you are effectively "burning off" the oil on the surface of the wok. If you are worried about setting off your smoke alarm or filling the kitchen with smoke, you can also season the wok outside on the barbecue. Allow the wok to cool completely, then repeat the whole heating and wiping process twice more (three times in all). Your wok is now ready to use.

caring for your wok The smooth round shape of the wok makes it quite easy to clean – no awkward angles for food to stick in. After each use, wash the wok in hot, soapy water with a sponge or cloth – never scrub it with scourers, steel wool or harsh abrasives or you will remove the "seasoned" surface. If any food still proves difficult to remove, simply fill the wok with water and allow to soak for a while, until the food softens. After washing, dry the wok thoroughly by standing it over low heat for a few minutes, then rub or spray a thin film of cooking oil over the inside surface before storing, to avoid rust. With constant use, the inside surface of the wok will darken and become well seasoned. The older, more seasoned the wok becomes, the better it cooks!

stir-frying accessories There are a great number of accessories available for your wok, but none of them is absolutely essential, except perhaps a wok chan or spatula. This is a long-handled, metal, shovel-like utensil, used for lifting, tossing and stirring food. If your wok has a non-stick surface, you should use a wooden wok chan to avoid damaging the wok. Also useful is a wire tempura rack that clips to the inside edge of the wok to drain deep-fried food, a pair of metal or wooden tongs for lifting and turning, a pair of extra-long chopsticks for stirring, and a high-domed lid to fit your wok when steaming.

1 heavy gauge carbon steel non-stick wok **2** glass lid
3 carbon steel wok **4** non-stick silverstone cast alloy wok
5 wok chan **6** wok strainer **7** wok burner
8 stainless steel wok

stir-fry greens

Nothing adds an authentic touch to a stir-fry as much as Asian green vegetables. Here are three favourites and how to prepare them.

bok choy (also called pak choi) Both stems and leaves may be eaten. Wash thoroughly before using. Baby bok choy can be left whole or cut in half lengthways; trim base of stalks on larger bok choy and cut away tough outer leaves close to stalk. May be steamed or stir-fried.

choy sum Small yellow flowers, mild-tasting tender stems and leaves, all of which are eaten. Trim stems and steam or stir-fry.

be prepared ...

The Golden Rule for stir-frying is the same as the famous Boy Scout maxim – be prepared. It's no use heating the wok, then wandering to the pantry to check if you have any oyster sauce.

Read the recipe through first, assemble all your ingredients and prepare them for the wok. If you are marinating meat or poultry, try to allow at least three hours for the flavours to develop.

Prepare garlic, chilli and ginger, if using, and set aside. Chop all the vegetables as specified, keeping them a uniform size and thickness. Because of the short cooking time, recipes often call for vegies to be cut into thin even strips, like matchsticks. The aim is to achieve the same stir-frying time for all ingredients.

Assemble and measure all the sauce ingredients, including stock or water and any that need to be pre-mixed with cornflour and water.

This may seem like a whole lot of bother, but once the preparation is done, the meal is practically finished!

chinese broccoli (also called gai larn) Dark green leaves and small white flowers. Wash thoroughly; discard larger, outer leaves. Peel and split thicker stems. Stir-fry or steam and serve with oyster sauce.

preparing ingredients for the wok

onion Cut in half lengthways; peel and discard tough outer skin. Place, cut-side down, on chopping board; cut into wedges or slice thinly.

garlic Crush garlic with the flat side of a large knife to loosen the skin, then peel the skin from the clove. Crush in a garlic press or chop very finely.

chilli Cut chillies lengthways in half; scrape out seeds and membrane with the tip of a small knife. Flatten, skin-side down, on chopping board; cut into thin strips.

Hold strips firmly together and chop finely.

ginger Peel away skin using a vegetable peeler then grate as finely as possible.

lemon grass Remove and discard tough end and root. Quarter lengthways then chop finely.

carrots Cut diagonally into thin slices. Place three slices on top of each other and cut into matchstick-size strips. Prepare zucchini similarly.

capsicum Halve crossways; discard stem, seeds and membrane. Cut

lengthways in half; place, skin-side down, on a board. Press down to flatten; cut lengthways into thin strips. Hold strips firmly together and chop as desired.

meat For best results, wrap meat tightly in plastic wrap, then partly freeze it, before cutting into wafer-thin slices across the grain.

marinades If marinating uncooked meat, poultry or seafood, always be sure that any reserved marinade used for sauce or dressing is brought to a boil before serving.

basic stir-fry 1, 2, 3

Heat wok over high heat before adding oil. Add half the specified amount of oil, then swirl wok to coat inside surface. Stir-fry meat, poultry or seafood in batches over very high heat, making sure that food has enough room to move. Remove each batch as it is cooked and reheat wok before adding the next batch. As each batch is added, it should sizzle. If the temperature is too low or the wok is crowded, the food will stew in its own juices and become tough.

Heat wok again and add remainder of oil. Add chopped onion and stir-fry for a minute or two, lifting and moving onion about the wok. Next add crushed garlic, ginger and chilli (if using) and stir-fry a few seconds longer, continuing to move the food about the wok constantly. Now add chopped vegetables, adding the hardest ones first and cooking them a little before adding the softer ones. Save leafy vegetables until the very end of the cooking process.

When all the vegies are almost cooked (and remember, they should still be crunchy), return the meat, poultry or seafood to the wok, then stir in the flavourings, stock or sauce ingredients, heating only until the sauce boils. Leafy green vegetables, bean sprouts and chopped herbs are best added to an almost completed stir-fry, just taken off the heat. The residual heat of the other food in the wok will "cook" the greens perfectly without the risk of overcooking.

beef

Spicy tastes and saucy combinations are quickly put together for great main meals, while lighter recipes, such as warm beef and eggplant stir-fry salad, are perfect for a smart entree. Tender, lean cuts of beef are best for stir-frying; fillet and rump steak are first choice, while blade, rib-eye (scotch fillet), round and sirloin steak are also suitable, although not quite as tender. To bring out their flavour, slice as thinly as possible before cooking.

sesame beef and noodles

PREPARATION TIME 15 MINUTES (plus marinating time) • COOKING TIME 10 MINUTES

500g beef steak, sliced thinly
1 tablespoon peanut oil
1 teaspoon sesame oil
2 cloves garlic, crushed
750g fresh rice noodle sheets
300g broccoli, chopped coarsely
2 tablespoons sesame seeds
1/4 cup (60ml) oyster sauce
1/4 cup (60ml) mild sweet chilli sauce

1 Combine beef, oils and garlic in medium bowl. Cover; refrigerate 3 hours or overnight.

2 Separate noodle sheets; cut into 2cm strips.

3 Add broccoli to small saucepan of boiling water; drain.

4 Stir-fry beef mixture in heated wok or large frying pan, in batches, until beef is browned; remove from wok.

5 Stir-fry seeds until they pop.

6 Return beef to wok with noodles, broccoli and sauces; stir-fry until hot.

SERVES 4

per serving 17.4g fat; 2756kJ

beef sukiyaki

PREPARATION TIME 15 MINUTES • COOKING TIME 30 MINUTES

100g vermicelli pasta
1/4 cup (60ml) mirin (sweet sake)
1 cup (250ml) salt-reduced
 soy sauce
1/2 cup (125ml) water
1 tablespoon sugar
1 tablespoon peanut oil
400g beef steak, sliced thinly
1 clove garlic, crushed
1 medium carrot (120g),
 sliced thinly
150g oyster mushrooms
150g shimeji mushrooms
60g enoki mushrooms
125g firm tofu, cubed
125g bok choy, chopped roughly
1/4 medium chinese cabbage
 (200g), shredded
1/4 cup (50g) bamboo shoots,
 sliced thinly
2 green onions, chopped finely

1 Cook vermicelli in large
 saucepan of boiling water until
 tender; drain. Cut vermicelli
 into shorter lengths.

2 Add mirin, sauce, the water and
 sugar to small saucepan; simmer,
 uncovered, about 30 minutes
 or until slightly thickened.

3 Meanwhile heat oil in wok or
 large frying pan. Stir-fry
 combined beef and garlic, in
 batches, until beef is browned;
 remove from wok.

4 Stir-fry carrot and mushrooms.

5 Add tofu, bok choy and
 cabbage; stir-fry.

6 Return beef to wok with
 vermicelli, mirin mixture,
 bamboo shoots and onion;
 stir-fry until hot.

SERVES 4

per serving 11.3g fat; 1509kJ

beef and black bean stir-fry

PREPARATION TIME 10 MINUTES • COOKING TIME 10 MINUTES

1 tablespoon peanut oil
400g beef steak, sliced thinly
1 clove garlic, crushed
1 medium white onion (150g),
 sliced thinly
2 trimmed sticks celery (150g),
 sliced thinly
1 teaspoon cornflour
1/4 cup (60ml) black bean sauce
1 teaspoon teriyaki sauce

1 Heat oil in wok or large frying pan. Stir-fry combined beef and garlic, in batches, until beef is browned; remove from wok.

2 Stir-fry onion and celery.

3 Return beef to wok with blended cornflour and sauces; stir until mixture boils and thickens slightly.

SERVES 4

per serving 9.7g fat; 880kJ

beef and vegetables with herb pesto

PREPARATION TIME 25 MINUTES • COOKING TIME 15 MINUTES

1¹/₂ cups firmly packed fresh basil leaves
¹/₄ cup firmly packed fresh oregano leaves
¹/₃ cup (25g) grated parmesan cheese
¹/₃ cup (80ml) olive oil
¹/₄ cup (60ml) cream
2 cloves garlic, crushed
1 tablespoon balsamic vinegar
2 teaspoons water
400g beef steak, sliced thinly
20 baby carrots, halved lengthways
1 medium red capsicum (200g), chopped coarsely
1 medium yellow capsicum (200g), chopped coarsely
200g sugar snap peas
¹/₂ cup (125ml) beef stock

1 Blend or process herbs, cheese, ¹/₄ cup (60ml) of the oil, cream, one clove garlic, vinegar and the water until combined. Transfer mixture to small saucepan; stir over low heat, without boiling, until heated through.

2 Heat remaining oil in wok or large frying pan. Stir-fry beef and remaining garlic, in batches, until beef is browned; remove from wok.

3 Stir-fry carrot and capsicums.

4 Return beef mixture to wok with peas and stock; stir until hot.

5 Serve stir-fry topped with warm herb pesto.

SERVES 4

per serving 31.9g fat; 1893kJ

chinese beef and cabbage

PREPARATION TIME 30 MINUTES (plus marinating and standing time) • COOKING TIME 25 MINUTES

500g beef steak, sliced thinly
1 tablespoon grated fresh ginger
2 cloves garlic, crushed
1 teaspoon five spice powder
1 tablespoon dry sherry
1 teaspoon sambal oelek
2 tablespoons hoisin sauce
5 dried shiitake mushrooms
2 tablespoons peanut oil
2 medium white onions (300g),
    sliced thinly
2 medium carrots (240g), sliced thinly
1/2 medium daikon (400g), sliced thinly
250g snow peas, sliced thinly
1/2 medium chinese cabbage
    (600g), shredded
425g can baby corn spears, drained, halved
1/4 cup (60ml) rice wine vinegar
2 tablespoons sugar
1/2 cup finely chopped fresh
    coriander leaves
1/4 cup (35g) slivered almonds, toasted

1 Combine beef, ginger, garlic, spice,
   sherry, sambal oelek and sauce in
   medium bowl. Cover; refrigerate 3 hours
   or overnight.

2 Soak mushrooms in boiling water
   20 minutes; drain mushrooms. Discard
   stems; chop caps.

3 Heat half of the oil in wok or large
   frying pan. Stir-fry undrained beef
   mixture, in batches, until beef is
   browned; remove from wok.

4 Heat remaining oil in wok. Add
   mushrooms and onion; stir-fry.

5 Add carrot and daikon; stir-fry.

6 Add snow peas, cabbage and corn; stir-fry.

7 Return beef mixture to wok with
   remaining ingredients; stir-fry until
   sauce boils.

   SERVES 4

   per serving 24.2g fat; 2207kJ

ginger beef and watercress

PREPARATION TIME 20 MINUTES (plus marinating time) • COOKING TIME 15 MINUTES

500g beef steak, sliced thinly
3 teaspoons grated fresh ginger
1 clove garlic, crushed
1 small fresh red chilli,
  chopped finely
2 tablespoons green ginger wine
2 teaspoons grated lemon rind
2 tablespoons lemon juice
1 tablespoon peanut oil
1 medium yellow capsicum
  (200g), sliced thickly
150g kumara, sliced thinly
1 medium white onion (150g),
  sliced thickly
2 teaspoons cornflour
1/3 cup (80ml) water
2 cups (100g) firmly
  packed watercress

1 Combine beef, ginger, garlic, chilli, wine, rind and juice in medium bowl. Cover; refrigerate 3 hours or overnight.

2 Heat oil in wok or large frying pan. Stir-fry capsicum, kumara and onion; remove from wok.

3 Stir-fry beef mixture, in batches, until beef is browned.

4 Return beef mixture and vegetables to wok with blended cornflour and water; stir until mixture boils and thickens slightly. Stir in watercress.

SERVES 4

per serving 10.6g fat; 1121kJ

satay beef stir-fry

PREPARATION TIME 20 MINUTES • COOKING TIME 10 MINUTES

1/2 cup (130g) crunchy peanut butter
2 tablespoons soy sauce
1 teaspoon grated lemon rind
1 tablespoon lemon juice
1/2 teaspoon dried crushed chillies
1 clove garlic, crushed
3/4 cup (180ml) coconut milk
2 teaspoons brown sugar
1 medium brown onion (150g), chopped finely
1 teaspoon ground cumin
1 teaspoon ground turmeric
2 tablespoons finely chopped fresh coriander leaves
1 tablespoon peanut oil
500g beef steak, sliced thinly
2 tablespoons chopped unsalted roasted peanuts
230g can water chestnuts, drained, sliced thinly
125g oyster mushrooms, sliced thinly
4 green onions, sliced thickly

1 Combine peanut butter, half of the sauce, rind, juice, chilli, garlic, half of the coconut milk and sugar in small saucepan; stir over low heat, without boiling, until heated through.

2 Process onion, remaining soy sauce, spices and coriander until smooth.

3 Heat oil in wok or large frying pan; stir-fry combined beef and onion paste, in batches, until beef is browned.

4 Return beef mixture to wok with remaining coconut milk and remaining ingredients; stir until hot.

5 Serve stir-fry with warm peanut sauce.

SERVES 4

per serving 40g fat; 2430kJ

thai beef stir-fry

PREPARATION TIME 10 MINUTES • COOKING TIME 10 MINUTES

2 teaspoons peanut oil
500g minced beef
2 teaspoons thai red curry paste
1 medium red capsicum (200g),
**   sliced thinly**
1 cup (80g) bean sprouts
4 green onions, sliced thickly
¹/₃ cup (80ml) coconut milk
2 tablespoons lime juice
1 tablespoon fish sauce
2 tablespoons shredded fresh
**   mint leaves**
4 large lettuce leaves

1 Heat oil in wok or large frying pan. Stir-fry combined beef and paste, in batches, until beef is cooked; remove from wok.

2 Stir-fry capsicum.

3 Return beef mixture to wok. Add sprouts, onion, coconut milk, juice and sauce; stir until hot.

4 Stir in mint. Serve stir-fry in lettuce leaves.

SERVES 4

per serving 16g fat; 1144kJ

warm beef and
eggplant stir-fry salad

PREPARATION TIME 20 MINUTES (plus marinating time) • COOKING TIME 30 MINUTES

500g beef steak, sliced thinly
2 tablespoons soy sauce
2 cloves garlic, crushed
2 small fresh red chillies,
  chopped finely
1 large red capsicum
  (350g), quartered
3 finger eggplants (180g)
2 tablespoons olive oil
1 medium brown onion
  (150g), sliced thickly
2 tablespoons lemon juice
1/4 teaspoon sugar
120g rocket
150g small curly endive

1 Combine beef, sauce, garlic and chilli in medium bowl. Cover; refrigerate 3 hours or overnight.

2 Quarter capsicums, remove seeds and membranes. Grill, skin side up, until skin blisters and blackens. Remove skin; slice capsicum.

3 Halve eggplants lengthways; grill until browned.

4 Heat half of the oil in wok or large non-stick frying pan. Stir-fry beef mixture, in batches, until beef is browned; remove from wok.

5 Stir-fry capsicum, eggplant and onion.

6 Return beef mixture to wok with remaining oil, juice and sugar; stir-fry.

7 Remove from heat; stir in rocket and endive.

SERVES 4

per serving 15.5g fat; 1255kJ

beef and leeks with crispy rice noodles

PREPARATION TIME 15 MINUTES (plus marinating time) • COOKING TIME 20 MINUTES

500g beef steak, sliced thinly
1/2 teaspoon sesame oil
4cm piece fresh ginger (40g), sliced thinly
2 tablespoons dry sherry
1 tablespoon soy sauce
80g rice vermicelli noodles
vegetable oil for deep-frying
1 tablespoon vegetable oil, extra
2 medium leeks (700g), sliced thinly
2 medium carrots (240g), sliced thinly
2 trimmed sticks celery (150g), sliced thinly
2 teaspoons cornflour
1 cup (250ml) beef stock

1 Combine beef, sesame oil, ginger, sherry and sauce in medium bowl. Cover; refrigerate 3 hours or overnight.

2 Break noodles into pieces. Deep-fry in hot vegetable oil until puffed and crisp; drain on absorbent paper.

3 Heat extra vegetable oil in wok or large frying pan. Stir-fry beef mixture, in batches, until beef is browned; remove from wok.

4 Stir-fry leek.

5 Add carrot and celery; stir-fry.

6 Return beef mixture to wok with blended cornflour and stock; stir until mixture boils and thickens slightly. Serve stir-fry with rice noodles.

SERVES 4

per serving 12.6g fat; 1308kJ

three-capsicum steak

PREPARATION TIME 20 MINUTES • COOKING TIME 10 MINUTES

1 tablespoon peanut oil
500g beef steak, sliced thinly
2 cloves garlic, crushed
1 large brown onion (200g),
**   sliced thickly**
2 medium red capsicums (400g),
**   sliced thinly**
2 medium green capsicums
**   (400g), sliced thinly**
2 medium yellow capsicums
**   (400g), sliced thinly**
6 medium egg tomatoes
**   (450g), quartered**
1/4 cup (60ml) soy sauce

1 Heat oil in wok or large frying pan. Stir-fry combined beef and garlic, in batches, until beef is browned; remove from wok.

2 Stir-fry onion and capsicums.

3 Return beef to wok with tomato and sauce; stir-fry until hot.

SERVES 4

per serving 10.8g fat; 1205kJ

chilli beef with sesame noodles

PREPARATION TIME 15 MINUTES • COOKING TIME 25 MINUTES

200g egg noodles
2 tablespoons peanut oil
2 tablespoons sesame
  seeds, toasted
1 teaspoon sesame oil
2 medium red capsicums (400g),
  sliced thinly
1 medium white onion (150g),
  sliced thinly
1 clove garlic, crushed
1 tablespoon grated fresh ginger
500g beef steak, sliced thinly
2 tablespoons lemon juice
2 tablespoons mild sweet
  chilli sauce
230g can bamboo shoots, drained
2 teaspoons cornflour
1 cup (250ml) beef stock

1 Cook noodles in large saucepan of boiling water until just tender; drain. Stir in half of the peanut oil and seeds.

2 Heat remaining peanut oil and sesame oil in wok or large frying pan. Stir-fry capsicum, onion, garlic and ginger; remove from wok.

3 Stir-fry beef, in batches, until browned.

4 Add capsicum mixture to wok with juice, sauce, bamboo shoots and blended cornflour and stock; stir until mixture boils and thickens slightly.

5 Serve stir-fry with noodles.

SERVES 4

per serving 20.8g fat; 1990kJ

italian beef sausage stir-fry

PREPARATION TIME 15 MINUTES • COOKING TIME 15 MINUTES (plus cooling time)

400g thin italian sausages
1 tablespoon olive oil
200g button mushrooms
2 small red onions (200g), sliced thinly
1 clove garlic, crushed
150g snow peas, sliced thickly
$1/2$ cup (75g) drained sun-dried tomatoes, sliced thickly
$1/2$ cup (60g) seeded black olives
$1/2$ cup (40g) grated parmesan cheese
$1/4$ cup finely shredded fresh basil leaves
$1/2$ cup (125ml) cream
$1/2$ cup (125ml) beef stock
2 egg yolks

1 Bring sausages to a boil in large saucepan of water; drain. Cool sausages 10 minutes; slice thickly.

2 Heat oil in wok or large frying pan. Stir-fry sausages until browned; remove from wok.

3 Stir-fry mushrooms, onion and garlic.

4 Return sausages to wok. Add snow peas, tomato, olives, cheese, basil, cream and stock; stir until mixture thickens slightly.

5 Remove from heat; stir in yolks.

SERVES 4

per serving 58.7g fat; 2998kJ

beef with pine nuts and cabbage

PREPARATION TIME 10 MINUTES • COOKING TIME 15 MINUTES

1 tablespoon peanut oil
500g beef steak, sliced thinly
2 cloves garlic, crushed
1 teaspoon sambal oelek
1 medium red capsicum
   (200g), sliced thinly
1/4 cup (40g) pine nuts
2 teaspoons oyster sauce
2 teaspoons cornflour
3/4 cup (180ml) beef stock
4 green onions, sliced thinly
1/4 medium chinese cabbage
   (200g), shredded

1 Heat oil in wok or large frying pan. Stir-fry combined beef, garlic and sambal oelek, in batches, until beef is browned; remove from wok.

2 Stir-fry capsicum and pine nuts.

3 Return beef to wok with sauce and blended cornflour and stock; stir until mixture boils and thickens slightly.

4 Add onion and cabbage; stir-fry until hot.

SERVES 4

per serving 17.8g fat; 1275J

chilli beef and spinach

PREPARATION TIME 10 MINUTES (plus marinating time) • COOKING TIME 10 MINUTES

400g beef steak, sliced thinly
1 tablespoon peanut oil
2 small fresh red chillies,
   chopped finely
1 clove garlic, crushed
500g english spinach,
   chopped thickly
2 teaspoons teriyaki sauce
1 teaspoon sugar
1 teaspoon cornflour
1/4 cup (60ml) beef stock

1 Combine beef, oil, chilli and garlic in medium bowl. Cover; refrigerate
   3 hours or overnight.

2 Stir-fry beef mixture in heated wok or large frying pan, in batches, until
   beef is browned; return beef to wok.

3 Add spinach, sauce and sugar to wok; stir-fry.

4 Add blended cornflour and stock; stir until sauce boils and thickens.

SERVES 4

per serving 9.4g fat; 798kJ

sichuan beef with cellophane noodles

PREPARATION TIME 20 MINUTES (plus marinating and standing time)
COOKING TIME 20 MINUTES

500g beef steak, sliced thinly
1/2 teaspoon sesame oil
1 teaspoon soy sauce
1 teaspoon fish sauce
1 teaspoon sugar
2 teaspoons sichuan pepper
1 tablespoon grated fresh ginger
1 tablespoon dry sherry
150g cellophane noodles
1 tablespoon peanut oil
1 medium white onion (150g), chopped finely
3 cloves garlic, crushed
1 trimmed stick celery (75g), sliced thinly
2 medium carrots (240g), sliced thinly
230g can sliced bamboo shoots, drained
300g snow peas, chopped coarsely
1 tablespoon oyster sauce
2 teaspoons cornflour
1/3 cup (80ml) water
1/4 cup finely shredded fresh basil leaves

1 Combine beef, sesame oil, soy sauce, fish sauce, sugar, pepper, ginger and sherry in medium bowl. Cover; refrigerate 3 hours or overnight.

2 Soak noodles in boiling water 3 minutes or until soft; drain. Cut into shorter lengths with scissors.

3 Heat peanut oil in wok or large frying pan. Stir-fry beef mixture, in batches, until beef is browned; remove from wok.

4 Stir-fry onion and garlic.

5 Add celery and carrot; stir-fry.

6 Add bamboo shoots and snow peas; stir-fry.

7 Return beef mixture to wok with oyster sauce and blended cornflour and water; stir until mixture boils and thickens slightly. Stir in basil.

SERVES 4

per serving 11.3g fat; 1617kJ

lamb

It only takes a few minutes to put together these wonderful stir-fries using lamb. Among them are treats you'd never expect could be cooked in a wok, such as pasta, altogether giving you a terrific choice of delicious main meals, entrees and lunches. Cuts perfect for stir-frying include trim lamb strips, lamb fillets, eye of loin, and leg and shoulder lamb.

lamb with honeyed garlic vegetables

PREPARATION TIME 15 MINUTES • COOKING TIME 20 MINUTES

2 tablespoons peanut oil
400g lamb fillets, sliced thinly
1 clove garlic, crushed
3 finger eggplants (180g), sliced thinly
1 medium white onion (150g), sliced thinly
1 medium carrot (120g), sliced thinly
1 medium red capsicum (200g), sliced thinly
425g can baby corn, drained
100g snow peas
1 tablespoon honey
1 teaspoon sugar
1 tablespoon cornflour
2 tablespoons oyster sauce
1 tablespoon soy sauce

1 Heat half of the oil in wok or large frying pan. Stir-fry combined lamb and garlic, in batches, until lamb is browned; remove from wok.

2 Heat remaining oil in wok; stir-fry eggplant and onion.

3 Add carrot and capsicum; stir-fry.

4 Add corn and snow peas; stir-fry.

5 Return lamb mixture to wok with honey, sugar and blended cornflour and sauces; stir until mixture boils and thickens.

SERVES 4

per serving 13.9g fat; 1409kJ

spinach and lamb with vegetable chunks

PREPARATION TIME 30 MINUTES • COOKING TIME 30 MINUTES

500g butternut pumpkin, cubed
4 small potatoes (480g),
   sliced thickly
1 medium red capsicum
   (200g), quartered
60g soft butter
2 tablespoons pine nuts, toasted
1 clove garlic, crushed
1/2 cup firmly packed fresh
   parsley sprigs
1 teaspoon cracked
   black peppercorns
1 tablespoon lemon juice
2 teaspoons olive oil
400g lamb fillets, sliced thinly
500g english spinach,
   chopped roughly

1 Boil, steam or microwave pumpkin and potato, separately, until just tender; drain.

2 Remove seeds and membranes from capsicum. Grill, skin side up, until skin blisters and blackens. Cover capsicum pieces with plastic or paper for 5 minutes. Remove skin; slice capsicum coarsely.

3 Process capsicum, butter, pine nuts, garlic, parsley, peppercorns and juice until combined.

4 Heat oil in wok or large frying pan. Stir-fry lamb, in batches, until browned; return lamb to wok.

5 Add pumpkin, potato, capsicum mixture and spinach; stir until spinach is just wilted.

SERVES 4

per serving 23.4g fat; 1792kJ

chilli lamb with peanut coconut sauce

PREPARATION TIME 20 MINUTES (plus marinating time) • COOKING TIME 25 MINUTES

500g trim lamb strips
2 small fresh red chillies,
  chopped finely
2 cloves garlic, crushed
4 cloves
1/2 teaspoon sesame oil
2 tablespoons teriyaki sauce
10 baby new potatoes
  (400g), halved
2 tablespoons vegetable oil
1 medium white onion
  (150g), sliced thickly
1/2 teaspoon ground turmeric
11/2 cups (375ml) coconut milk
1/2 cup (75g) unsalted
  roasted peanuts
3 green onions, chopped roughly

1 Combine lamb, chilli, garlic, cloves, sesame oil and sauce in large bowl. Cover; refrigerate 3 hours or overnight.

2 Boil, steam or microwave potato until just tender; drain.

3 Heat half of the vegetable oil in wok or large frying pan. Stir-fry combined potato, white onion and turmeric, in batches, until onion is soft; remove from wok.

4 Heat remaining vegetable oil in wok; stir-fry lamb mixture, in batches, until lamb is browned.

5 Return lamb and potato mixture to wok with coconut milk, peanuts and green onion; stir-fry until hot.

SERVES 4

per serving 43.7g fat; 2646kJ

creamy lamb and linguine with mint pesto

PREPARATION TIME 15 MINUTES • COOKING TIME 25 MINUTES

500g linguine
2 cups firmly packed fresh mint leaves
2 cloves garlic, crushed
1/3 cup (50g) pine nuts
2 tablespoons grated parmesan cheese
1/3 cup (80ml) light olive oil
3 teaspoons sugar
500g lamb fillets, sliced thinly
300ml cream

1 Cook linguine in large saucepan of boiling water, uncovered, until just tender; drain.

2 Process mint, garlic, pine nuts, cheese, 1/4 cup (60ml) of the oil and sugar until combined.

3 Heat remaining oil in wok or large frying pan. Stir-fry lamb, in batches, until browned; remove from wok.

4 Combine mint pesto and cream in wok; stir well.

5 Return lamb and linguine to wok; stir-fry until hot.

SERVES 4

per serving 67.3g fat; 4879kJ

ginger, honey and yogurt lamb

PREPARATION TIME 20 MINUTES (plus marinating time) • COOKING TIME 10 MINUTES

500g lamb fillets, sliced thinly
1/3 cup (95g) plain yogurt
2 cloves garlic, crushed
1 tablespoon grated fresh ginger
2 tablespoons honey
1 teaspoon ground turmeric
2 teaspoons cumin seeds
1 tablespoon vegetable oil
2 trimmed sticks celery (150g), sliced thinly
1 large red capsicum (350g), sliced thinly
1 large brown onion (200g), sliced thinly
3 teaspoons finely chopped fresh thyme

1 Combine lamb, yogurt, garlic, ginger, honey, turmeric and cumin in medium bowl. Cover; refrigerate 3 hours or overnight.

2 Heat half of the oil in wok or large frying pan. Stir-fry celery, capsicum, onion and thyme; remove from wok. Cover to keep warm.

3 Heat remaining oil in wok; stir-fry undrained lamb mixture, in batches, until lamb is browned.

4 Serve lamb with celery mixture.

SERVES 4

per serving 10.3g fat; 1183kJ

chilli lamb with coconut cream and coriander

PREPARATION TIME 15 MINUTES • COOKING TIME 15 MINUTES

1 tablespoon peanut oil
2 small fresh red chillies,
  chopped finely
1 clove garlic, crushed
2 teaspoons grated fresh ginger
1 medium brown onion (150g),
  sliced thinly
450g lamb fillets, sliced thinly
1 tablespoon fish sauce
2 teaspoons sugar
3/4 cup (180ml) coconut cream
2 tablespoons finely chopped
  fresh coriander leaves

1 Heat oil in wok or large frying pan. Stir-fry chilli, garlic, ginger and onion until onion is soft; remove from wok.

2 Stir-fry lamb, in batches, until browned.

3 Return lamb and onion mixture to wok with sauce, sugar, coconut cream and coriander; stir-fry until hot.

SERVES 4

per serving 18g fat; 1197kJ

lamb with sage

PREPARATION TIME 15 MINUTES (plus marinating time)
COOKING TIME 15 MINUTES

500g trim lamb strips
1 clove garlic, crushed
1/4 teaspoon dried crushed chillies
2 tablespoons balsamic vinegar
2 tablespoons olive oil
1 medium yellow capsicum (200g), sliced thinly
1 medium red onion (170g), sliced thinly
425g can tomatoes
1/2 cup (75g) pimiento-stuffed green olives
1 1/2 tablespoons finely chopped fresh sage

1 Combine lamb, garlic, chilli and vinegar in medium bowl. Cover; refrigerate 3 hours or overnight.

2 Heat half of the oil in wok or large frying pan. Stir-fry undrained lamb mixture, in batches, until lamb is browned; remove from wok.

3 Heat remaining oil in wok; stir-fry capsicum and onion.

4 Return lamb to wok with undrained crushed tomatoes and remaining ingredients; stir-fry until hot.

SERVES 4

per serving 15.5g fat; 1186kJ

chickpea and lamb curry

PREPARATION TIME 15 MINUTES • COOKING TIME 15 MINUTES

1 tablespoon vegetable oil
1 clove garlic, crushed
1 teaspoon ground cinnamon
1 teaspoon ground cumin
1/2 teaspoon ground cardamom
400g lamb fillets, sliced thinly
**1 medium white onion (150g),
  sliced thinly**
150g green beans, halved
310g can chickpeas, drained
**2 small tomatoes (260g),
  chopped coarsely**
**500g english spinach,
  chopped coarsely**
1 teaspoon cornflour
2/3 cup (160ml) beef stock

1 Heat oil in wok or large frying pan; stir-fry garlic and spices until fragrant.

2 Add lamb to wok, in batches. Stir-fry until lamb is browned; remove from wok.

3 Stir-fry onion and beans.

4 Return lamb to wok with chickpeas, tomato, spinach, blended cornflour and stock; stir-fry until mixture boils and thickens slightly.

SERVES 4

per serving 10g fat; 1053kJ

mediterranean lamb stir-fry

PREPARATION TIME 25 MINUTES (plus marinating time) • COOKING TIME 15 MINUTES

400g trim lamb strips
1/4 cup (60ml) dry red wine
2 cloves garlic, crushed
1 tablespoon brown sugar
2 teaspoons Worcestershire sauce
2 medium red capsicums
  (400g), quartered
2 tablespoons olive oil
3 small eggplants (690g),
  chopped coarsely
1 small fennel bulb (300g),
  sliced thickly
6 slices prosciutto (90g),
  sliced thinly
1 tablespoon finely chopped fresh
  oregano leaves
1/2 cup (125ml) water

1 Combine lamb, wine, garlic, sugar and sauce in medium bowl. Cover; refrigerate 3 hours or overnight.

2 Remove seeds and membranes from capsicum. Grill, skin side up, until skin blisters and blackens. Remove skin; slice capsicum.

3 Heat half of the oil in wok or large frying pan. Stir-fry eggplant, fennel and prosciutto; remove from wok.

4 Heat remaining oil; stir-fry undrained lamb mixture, in batches, until lamb is browned.

5 Return lamb and eggplant mixture to wok with capsicum, oregano and the water; stir-fry until hot.

SERVES 4

per serving 14.8g fat; 1322kJ

quick lamb curry with mango relish

PREPARATION TIME 30 MINUTES (plus marinating time)
COOKING TIME 20 MINUTES

500g lamb fillets, sliced thinly
1 tablespoon grated fresh ginger
2 cloves garlic, crushed
1/4 cup (75g) madras curry paste
1 medium mango (430g), chopped coarsely
1 tablespoon finely chopped fresh coriander leaves
2 teaspoons white wine vinegar
1/2 teaspoon mild sweet chilli sauce
2 tablespoons vegetable oil
1 medium white onion (150g), sliced thickly
1 teaspoon black mustard seeds
2 teaspoons cornflour
1/2 cup (125ml) beef stock
1/3 cup (95g) plain yogurt

1 Combine lamb, ginger, garlic and paste in medium bowl. Cover; refrigerate 3 hours or overnight.

2 Combine mango, coriander, vinegar and sauce in separate bowl.

3 Heat one-quarter of the oil in wok or large frying pan. Stir-fry onion and seeds until onion is soft; remove from wok.

4 Heat remaining oil in wok; stir-fry lamb mixture, in batches, until browned.

5 Return lamb and onion mixtures to wok with blended cornflour, stock and yogurt; stir until mixture boils and thickens slightly.

6 Serve curry with mango relish.

SERVES 4

per serving 20.2g fat; 1522kJ

curried lamb and vegetables

PREPARATION TIME 15 MINUTES • COOKING TIME 20 MINUTES

2 tablespoons peanut oil
150g green beans, halved
1 medium carrot (120g),
** sliced thinly**
1 large red capsicum (350g),
** sliced thinly**
425g can baby corn, drained
1 teaspoon sesame oil
1 clove garlic, crushed
2 teaspoons curry powder
400g lamb fillets, sliced thinly
1 teaspoon cornflour
1/2 cup (125ml) chicken stock
2 teaspoons soy sauce

1 Heat half of the peanut oil in wok or large frying pan; stir-fry beans.

2 Add carrot, capsicum and corn to wok. Stir-fry; remove vegetables from wok.

3 Heat remaining peanut oil and sesame oil in wok; stir-fry garlic and curry powder until fragrant.

4 Add lamb to wok, in batches; stir-fry until browned.

5 Return lamb and vegetable mixture to wok with blended cornflour, stock and sauce; stir until mixture boils and thickens slightly.

SERVES 4

per serving 15.1g fat; 1277kJ

lamb with tomatoes, fetta and olives

PREPARATION TIME 15 MINUTES (plus marinating time) • COOKING TIME 15 MINUTES

500g lamb fillets, sliced thinly
2 tablespoons olive oil
2 cloves garlic, crushed
1 teaspoon cracked
 black peppercorns
1 teaspoon grated lemon rind
2 tablespoons lemon juice
1 tablespoon finely chopped
 fresh oregano leaves
250g green beans, halved
1 medium white onion
 (150g), quartered
250g cherry tomatoes
1 cup (160g) black olives
200g fetta cheese, cubed

1 Combine lamb, half of the oil, garlic, peppercorns, rind, juice and oregano in medium bowl. Cover; refrigerate 3 hours or overnight.

2 Add beans to large saucepan of boiling water; drain. Rinse under cold water; drain.

3 Stir-fry lamb mixture in heated wok or large frying pan, in batches, until lamb is browned; remove from wok.

4 Heat remaining oil in wok; stir-fry beans and onion.

5 Return lamb mixture to wok with remaining ingredients; stir-fry until hot.

SERVES 4

per serving 25.9g fat; 1819kJ

poultry

We have dipped freely into different cuisines to create these fresh, delightful dishes using chicken and duck. Some, such as duck with oranges and vermouth, make a pretty entree, but all are great as main courses, if preferred. The best cuts are tender chicken and duck breast fillets, or chicken thigh fillets and tenderloins.

mango and macadamia chicken

PREPARATION TIME 15 MINUTES (plus marinating time)
COOKING TIME 15 MINUTES

500g chicken thigh fillets, sliced thinly
2 tablespoons dry white wine
1 clove garlic, crushed
1 small fresh red chilli, seeded, chopped finely
1 tablespoon finely chopped fresh basil leaves
2 tablespoons olive oil
2 medium red onions (340g), sliced thinly
2 medium yellow capsicums (400g), sliced thinly
1 medium red capsicum (200g), sliced thinly
2 medium mangoes (860g), sliced thinly
1/4 cup (35g) chopped macadamias, toasted
240g rocket

1 Combine chicken, wine, garlic, chilli, basil and half of the oil in medium bowl. Cover; refrigerate 3 hours or overnight.

2 Heat half of the remaining oil in wok or large frying pan. Stir-fry chicken mixture, in batches, until chicken is browned; remove from wok.

3 Heat remaining oil in wok; stir-fry onion and capsicums.

4 Return chicken mixture to wok; add mango and nuts. Remove from heat; add rocket.

SERVES 4

per serving 25.8g fat; 2003kJ

chicken and cashews with broccoli

PREPARATION TIME 10 MINUTES • COOKING TIME 10 MINUTES

2 tablespoons vegetable oil
500g chicken thigh fillets,
   chopped coarsely
1 clove garlic, crushed
1 small leek (200g), sliced thinly
1 medium carrot (120g),
   sliced thinly
250g broccoli, chopped coarsely
1 teaspoon cornflour
1/2 cup (125ml) chicken stock
2 tablespoons oyster sauce
1/2 cup (75g) unsalted
   roasted cashews

1 Heat half of the oil in wok or large frying pan. Stir-fry chicken, in batches, until browned; remove from wok.

2 Heat remaining oil in wok; stir-fry garlic, leek, carrot and broccoli until leek is soft.

3 Return chicken to wok with blended cornflour and stock, sauce and nuts; stir until mixture boils and thickens slightly.

SERVES 4

per serving 28.3g fat; 1758kJ

chicken kumara stir-fry

PREPARATION TIME 15 MINUTES • COOKING TIME 20 MINUTES

2 tablespoons vegetable oil
500g chicken thigh fillets,
  chopped coarsely
1 clove garlic, crushed
1 medium brown onion (150g),
  chopped coarsely
1 small kumara (250g),
  chopped coarsely
250g silverbeet, chopped roughly
1/2 teaspoon sesame oil
1 teaspoon cornflour
1 cup (250ml) chicken stock

1 Heat half of the vegetable oil in wok or large frying pan. Stir-fry chicken, in batches, until browned; remove from wok.

2 Heat remaining vegetable oil in wok; stir-fry garlic, onion and kumara until kumara is just tender.

3 Return chicken to wok. Add silverbeet, sesame oil and blended cornflour and stock; stir until mixture boils and thickens slightly.

SERVES 4

per serving 19g fat; 1337kJ

garlic and chilli chicken with basil

PREPARATION TIME 10 MINUTES (plus marinating time)
COOKING TIME 15 MINUTES

600g chicken breast fillets, sliced thickly
2 cloves garlic, crushed
1 small fresh red chilli, sliced thinly
1 small fresh green chilli, sliced thinly
2 tablespoons lemon juice
1/4 cup (60ml) oyster sauce
2 tablespoons olive oil
2 medium white onions (300g), sliced thickly
1 large red capsicum (350g), chopped coarsely
2 teaspoons cornflour
1 cup (250ml) chicken stock
1/4 cup firmly packed fresh basil leaves
4 green onions, sliced thinly

1 Combine chicken, garlic, chillies, juice and sauce in medium bowl. Cover; refrigerate 3 hours or overnight.

2 Heat half of the oil in wok or large frying pan. Stir-fry chicken mixture, in batches, until chicken is browned; remove from wok.

3 Heat remaining oil in wok; stir-fry white onion and capsicum until onion is just soft.

4 Return chicken mixture to wok with blended cornflour and stock; stir until mixture boils and thickens slightly. Stir in basil and green onion.

SERVES 4

per serving 16.2g fat; 1391kJ

teriyaki chicken with green beans

PREPARATION TIME 20 MINUTES (plus marinating time) • COOKING TIME 15 MINUTES

**500g chicken breast fillets,
sliced thinly**
2 tablespoons black bean sauce
**1 tablespoon mild sweet
chilli sauce**
1 tablespoon teriyaki sauce
1 clove garlic, crushed
2 teaspoons grated fresh ginger
**1 medium white onion (150g),
sliced thinly**
1 tablespoon peanut oil
200g green beans, halved
1/4 cup (60ml) water
400g bok choy, sliced thickly
1 1/4 cups (100g) bean sprouts

1 Combine chicken, sauces, garlic, ginger and onion in medium bowl. Cover; refrigerate 3 hours or overnight.

2 Drain chicken; reserve marinade

3 Heat oil in wok or large frying pan. Stir-fry chicken mixture, in batches, until browned; return chicken to wok.

4 Add beans and the water; stir until beans are tender.

5 Add bok choy and sprouts; stir until hot.

SERVES 4

per serving 12.3g fat; 1144kJ

chicken with ginger and lemon grass

PREPARATION TIME 15 MINUTES (plus marinating time) • COOKING TIME 15 MINUTES

500g chicken breast fillets,
  chopped coarsely
1 teaspoon sesame oil
2 tablespoons peanut oil
1 clove garlic, crushed
1 tablespoon grated fresh ginger
2 teaspoons finely chopped
  fresh lemon grass
1/3 cup (80ml) white vinegar
2 teaspoons soy sauce
2 teaspoons sugar
200g broccoli, chopped coarsely
1 large red capsicum (300g),
  sliced thinly
5 green onions, sliced thickly

1 Combine chicken, oils, garlic, ginger, lemon grass, vinegar, sauce and sugar in medium bowl. Cover; refrigerate 3 hours or overnight.

2 Stir-fry chicken mixture in heated wok or large frying pan, in batches, until chicken is browned; remove from wok.

3 Stir-fry broccoli and capsicum 1 minute.

4 Return chicken mixture to wok. Add onion; stir-fry until hot.

SERVES 4

per serving 17.4g fat; 1313kJ

sweet and sour chicken

PREPARATION TIME 30 MINUTES (plus marinating time) • COOKING TIME 20 MINUTES

400g chicken tenderloins
2 cloves garlic, crushed
2 teaspoons grated fresh ginger
1 tablespoon soy sauce
2 teaspoons peanut oil
250g button mushrooms, quartered
1 small pineapple (800g), peeled,
**   chopped coarsely**
3 teaspoons cornflour
³/₄ cup (180ml) chicken stock
¹/₄ cup (60ml) tomato sauce
2 tablespoons brown malt vinegar
1 tablespoon brown sugar
80g snow pea sprouts

1 Combine chicken, garlic, ginger and soy sauce in medium bowl. Cover; refrigerate 3 hours or overnight.

2 Heat oil in wok or large frying pan. Stir-fry chicken mixture, in batches, until chicken is browned; remove from wok.

3 Stir-fry mushrooms.

4 Add pineapple, blended cornflour and stock, tomato sauce, vinegar and sugar; stir until mixture boils and thickens slightly.

5 Return chicken mixture to wok. Add sprouts; stir until hot.

SERVES 4

per serving 8.4g fat; 1164kJ

chicken with spicy mango sauce

PREPARATION TIME 10 MINUTES (plus marinating time) • COOKING TIME 15 MINUTES

500g chicken thigh fillets,
sliced thinly
1 tablespoon mild curry paste
1 tablespoon lime juice
1 tablespoon peanut oil
300g broccoli, chopped coarsely
150g snow peas
1/2 cup (125ml) chicken stock
1 cup (250ml) coconut milk
1 tablespoon mango chutney
1 medium mango (430g),
sliced thickly
1/3 cup (15g) flaked
coconut, toasted
1/4 cup coarsely chopped fresh
coriander leaves

1 Combine chicken, paste and juice in medium bowl. Cover; refrigerate 3 hours or overnight.

2 Heat oil in wok or large frying pan. Stir-fry chicken mixture, in batches, until chicken is browned; return chicken to wok.

3 Add broccoli, peas, stock, coconut milk and chutney; stir until sauce boils.

4 Add mango; stir until hot. Serve sprinkled with coconut and coriander.

SERVES 4

per serving 29.8g fat; 1911kJ

duck with oranges and vermouth

PREPARATION TIME 20 MINUTES (plus marinating time)
COOKING TIME 15 MINUTES

500g duck breast fillets
$1^1/_2$ cups (375ml) orange juice
$^3/_4$ cup (180ml) vermouth
2 tablespoons teriyaki sauce
1 teaspoon cracked black peppercorns
2 cloves garlic, crushed
3 small kumara (750g), chopped coarsely
2 tablespoons peanut oil
2 medium red onions (340g), sliced thinly
2 teaspoons cornflour
150g mixed salad leaves
1 medium orange (240g), peeled, chopped coarsely

1 Combine duck, juice, vermouth, sauce, peppercorns and garlic in medium bowl. Cover; refrigerate 3 hours or overnight.

2 Drain duck from marinade; reserve marinade.

3 Boil, steam or microwave kumara until just tender; drain.

4 Heat oil in wok or large frying pan. Stir-fry kumara and onion until onion is soft; remove from wok. Cover to keep warm.

5 Stir-fry duck, in batches, until duck is browned; remove from wok. Cover to keep warm.

6 Pour blended cornflour and reserved marinade into wok; stir until sauce boils and thickens slightly.

7 Place salad leaves, kumara mixture, duck and orange on serving plate; pour sauce over top.

SERVES 4

per serving 13g fat; 1630kJ

warm chicken and pecan salad

PREPARATION TIME 15 MINUTES • COOKING TIME 15 MINUTES

1/4 cup (60ml) olive oil
2 tablespoons lemon juice
pinch sugar
1 teaspoon seeded mustard
1 clove garlic, crushed
1 tablespoon cream
2 teaspoons olive oil, extra
400g chicken breast fillets,
    sliced thinly
2 bacon rashers, chopped roughly
1 trimmed stick celery (75g),
    sliced thinly
4 green onions, sliced thickly
1/2 cup (50g) pecans, toasted
100g mixed salad leaves
1 medium avocado (250g),
    sliced thinly
100g camembert cheese,
    sliced thinly
1 tablespoon coarsely chopped
    fresh chives

1 Combine oil, juice, sugar, mustard, garlic and cream in screw-top jar; shake well.

2 Heat extra oil in wok or large frying pan. Stir-fry chicken, in batches, until browned; remove from wok.

3 Stir-fry bacon until crisp.

4 Return chicken to wok with celery, onion and nuts; stir-fry.

5 Serve salad leaves topped with chicken mixture, avocado and cheese.

6 Drizzle with dressing; sprinkle with chives.

SERVES 4

per serving 50.8g fat; 2494kJ

spicy chicken and coconut

PREPARATION TIME 15 MINUTES • COOKING TIME 15 MINUTES

2 tablespoons peanut oil
660g chicken thigh fillets,
**   chopped coarsely**
2 medium white onions (300g),
**   sliced thickly**
1 large red capsicum (350g),
**   chopped coarsely**
400ml coconut milk
¼ cup (75g) red curry paste
1 tablespoon fish sauce
¼ cup shredded fresh basil leaves

1 Heat 2 teaspoons of the oil in wok or large frying pan. Stir-fry chicken, in batches, until browned; remove from wok.

2 Heat remaining oil in wok; stir-fry onion and capsicum until onion is just soft.

3 Return chicken to wok with coconut milk, paste and sauce; stir until mixture boils. Stir in basil.

SERVES 4

per serving 44.3g fat; 2480kJ

honey duck

PREPARATION TIME 30 MINUTES (plus marinating time) • COOKING TIME 25 MINUTES (plus cooling time)

500g duck breast fillets
2 cloves garlic, crushed
3 teaspoons grated fresh ginger
1 teaspoon five spice powder
2 small fresh red chillies,
  chopped finely
2 tablespoons dry sherry
1/4 cup (60ml) honey
1/4 cup (60ml) salt-reduced
  soy sauce
3 small carrots (210g),
  sliced thinly
1 tablespoon peanut oil
6 green onions, sliced thickly
250g snow peas
1 teaspoon cornflour
2 tablespoons water
2 cups (100g) firmly
  packed watercress

1 Combine duck, garlic, ginger, spice powder, chilli, sherry, honey and half of the sauce in medium bowl. Cover; refrigerate 3 hours or overnight.

2 Drain duck from marinade; reserve marinade. Grill duck, skin side up, until skin is brown and crisp; cool. Slice duck thinly.

3 Add carrot to medium saucepan of boiling water. Boil 1 minute; drain. Rinse under cold water; drain.

4 Heat half of the oil in wok or large frying pan. Stir-fry reserved marinade and duck, in batches, until marinade boils; remove from wok.

5 Clean wok.

6 Heat remaining oil in wok; stir-fry carrot, onion and snow peas 1 minute.

7 Add blended cornflour and water and remaining sauce; stir until sauce boils and thickens slightly.

8 Return duck mixture to wok. Add watercress; stir-fry until hot.

SERVES 4

per serving 8.2g fat; 981kJ

chicken tikka stir-fry

PREPARATION TIME 10 MINUTES (plus marinating time) • COOKING TIME 15 MINUTES

500g chicken thigh fillets, sliced thinly
1/4 cup (75g) tikka paste
1 tablespoon vegetable oil
2 medium yellow capsicums (400g), chopped coarsely
160g snow pea sprouts
1/4 cup (70g) plain yogurt

1 Combine chicken and paste in medium bowl. Cover; refrigerate 3 hours or overnight.

2 Heat oil in wok or large frying pan. Stir-fry chicken mixture, in batches, until chicken is browned; remove from wok.

3 Stir-fry capsicum until just tender.

4 Return chicken and sprouts to wok; stir-fry until sprouts are just wilted.

5 Add yogurt; stir until hot.

SERVES 4

per serving 19.9g fat; 1473kJ

chicken and water chestnuts in lettuce cups

PREPARATION TIME 25 MINUTES (plus soaking time)
COOKING TIME 20 MINUTES

5 dried shiitake mushrooms
2 tablespoons vegetable oil
500g minced chicken
1/4 teaspoon sesame oil
1 small red capsicum (150g), chopped finely
2 cloves garlic, crushed
1 tablespoon grated fresh ginger
230g can bamboo shoots, drained, chopped finely
230g can water chestnuts, drained, chopped finely
4 green onions, sliced thinly
1 tablespoon soy sauce
1 tablespoon oyster sauce
1 tablespoon dry sherry
1/3 cup (80ml) water
1/2 teaspoon sambal oelek
1 iceberg lettuce

1 Soak mushrooms in boiling water 20 minutes; drain mushrooms. Discard stems; slice caps finely.

2 Heat half of the vegetable oil in wok or large frying pan. Stir-fry chicken, in batches, until browned; remove from wok.

3 Heat remaining vegetable oil and sesame oil in wok; stir-fry capsicum, garlic and ginger.

4 Return chicken to wok with mushrooms, bamboo shoots, chestnuts, onion, sauces, sherry, the water and sambal oelek; stir until hot.

5 Serve in lettuce cups.

SERVES 4

per serving 20.3g fat; 1357kJ

fruity chicken with herbed couscous

PREPARATION TIME 15 MINUTES (plus marinating time) • COOKING TIME 10 MINUTES (plus standing time)

**600g chicken thigh fillets,
  chopped roughly**
¹/₄ cup (80g) fruit chutney
2 tablespoons dry white wine
1 tablespoon grated fresh ginger
1 clove garlic, crushed
1 teaspoon ground cumin
¹/₄ teaspoon dried crushed chillies
1¹/₄ cups (310ml) water
40g butter
1¹/₂ cups (300g) couscous
**2 tablespoons finely chopped
  fresh parsley**
2 tablespoons olive oil
**1 tablespoon finely chopped fresh
  oregano leaves**

1 Combine chicken, chutney, wine, ginger, garlic, cumin and chilli in medium bowl. Cover; refrigerate 3 hours or overnight.

2 Bring the water to a boil in large saucepan. Add butter and couscous; stir. Cover; stand 5 minutes or until water is absorbed. Stir in parsley.

3 Heat half of the oil in wok or large frying pan. Stir-fry chicken mixture, in batches, until chicken is browned; return chicken to wok.

4 Add oregano; stir until hot.

5 Serve with couscous.

SERVES 4

per serving 28.8g fat; 2849kJ

chicken with
sweet garlic eggplants

PREPARATION TIME 15 MINUTES (plus marinating time) • COOKING TIME 15 MINUTES

500g chicken breast fillets,
  chopped coarsely
2 cloves garlic, crushed
2 tablespoons teriyaki sauce
1 tablespoon soy sauce
1/4 cup (60ml) honey
2 tablespoons vegetable oil
6 finger eggplants (360g),
  sliced thickly
5 green onions, chopped coarsely
425g can baby corn, drained
1 tablespoon cornflour
2 tablespoons water

1 Combine chicken, garlic, sauces and honey in medium bowl. Cover; refrigerate 3 hours or overnight.

2 Heat half of the oil in wok or large frying pan. Stir-fry chicken mixture, in batches, until chicken is browned; remove from wok.

3 Heat remaining oil in wok. Stir-fry eggplant until browned.

4 Add onion; stir-fry 1 minute.

5 Return chicken to wok. Add corn and blended cornflour and water; stir until sauce boils and thickens.

SERVES 4

per serving 17.3g fat; 1758kJ

smoked chicken and fried noodle salad

PREPARATION TIME 15 MINUTES • COOKING TIME 15 MINUTES

500g asparagus, chopped coarsely
1/2 cup (125ml) lemon juice
1/2 cup (125ml) peanut oil
1 tablespoon sugar
3 teaspoons grated fresh ginger
1/4 cup finely chopped fresh coriander leaves
2 teaspoons peanut oil, extra
1 large kumara (500g), sliced thinly
250g smoked chicken breast fillet, sliced thinly
300g snow peas
8 green onions, sliced thickly
100g packaged fried noodles

1 Plunge asparagus into medium saucepan of boiling water; drain immediately.

2 Combine juice, oil, sugar, ginger and coriander in screw-top jar; shake well.

3 Heat extra oil in wok or large frying pan; stir-fry kumara until just tender.

4 Add asparagus, chicken, peas and onion; stir-fry until hot.

5 Stir in ginger mixture. Serve sprinkled with noodles.

SERVES 4

per serving 37.8g fat; 2341kJ

chicken with peppercorns

PREPARATION TIME 15 MINUTES • COOKING TIME 20 MINUTES

1 tablespoon vegetable oil
500g chicken breast fillets,
  sliced thinly
2 bacon rashers, chopped finely
1 medium red onion (170g),
  sliced thinly
1 medium zucchini (120g),
  sliced thinly
1 medium yellow capsicum
  (200g), sliced thinly
1 medium red capsicum (200g),
  sliced thinly
2 teaspoons drained
  green peppercorns
1 tablespoon dry white wine
1/2 cup (125ml) cream

1 Heat oil in wok or large frying pan. Stir-fry chicken, in batches, until browned; remove from wok.

2 Stir-fry bacon until crisp; remove from wok.

3 Stir-fry onion, zucchini and capsicums until onion is soft.

4 Return chicken and bacon to wok. Add peppercorns and wine; boil, stirring, 1 minute.

5 Add cream; stir until hot.

SERVES 4

per serving 27g fat; 1709kJ

chicken chow mein

PREPARATION TIME 35 MINUTES (plus marinating time) • COOKING TIME 25 MINUTES

**400g chicken thigh fillets,
   sliced thinly**
200g pork fillet, sliced thinly
1 clove garlic, crushed
2 tablespoons peanut oil
2 teaspoons soy sauce
1 teaspoon brandy
1 small carrot (70g), sliced thinly
**1 medium red capsicum (200g),
   sliced thinly**
4 green onions, chopped finely
**2 trimmed sticks celery (150g),
   sliced thinly**
**200g uncooked medium prawns,
   shelled, chopped coarsely**
**1/2 medium chinese cabbage
   (400g), shredded**
1 tablespoon oyster sauce
1 teaspoon cornflour
1/2 cup (125ml) chicken stock
100g packaged fried noodles

1 Combine chicken, pork, garlic, half of the oil, soy sauce and brandy in medium bowl. Cover; refrigerate 3 hours or overnight.

2 Heat half of the remaining oil in wok or large frying pan. Stir-fry chicken and pork mixture, in batches, until browned; remove from wok.

3 Heat remaining oil in wok; stir-fry carrot, capsicum, onion and celery until carrot is just tender.

4 Add prawns and cabbage; stir-fry until cabbage is almost wilted.

5 Return chicken mixture to wok with oyster sauce and blended cornflour and stock; stir until mixture boils and thickens slightly.

6 Serve with noodles.

SERVES 4

per serving 20.5g fat; 1643kJ

pork

We have used pork, a mainstay of Asian stir-fries, in recipes as diverse as the Chinese-influenced barbecued pork chow mein to quick ways with favourite western flavour combinations, such as pork and macadamia stir-fried salad. Also included are exciting new ways to use prosciutto. Pork leg strips, fillet and schnitzel are all ideal cuts for stir-frying. However, do not over-cook pork, or it will become dry and tough.

lemon and ginger pork ribs with plum sauce

PREPARATION TIME 30 MINUTES (plus marinating time)
COOKING TIME 15 MINUTES (plus cooling time)

1kg pork spare ribs
3/4 cup (180ml) plum sauce
2 tablespoons soy sauce
2 teaspoons grated lemon rind
2 teaspoons grated fresh ginger
1 tablespoon peanut oil
150g snow peas, halved

1 Cut each rib section into three pieces; place in large saucepan. Cover with cold water; bring to a boil. Drain; cool.

2 Combine ribs, sauces, rind and ginger in medium bowl. Cover; refrigerate 3 hours or overnight.

3 Heat oil in wok or large frying pan; stir-fry undrained rib mixture, in batches, until ribs are browned.

4 Return ribs to wok. Add snow peas; stir-fry until hot.

SERVES 4

per serving 13.4g fat; 1568kJ

chilli pork and noodles

PREPARATION TIME 20 MINUTES • COOKING TIME 30 MINUTES

375g thick fresh egg noodles
1 teaspoon peanut oil
2 eggs, beaten lightly
1 tablespoon peanut oil, extra
450g minced pork
2 teaspoons grated fresh ginger
2 cloves garlic, crushed
2 tablespoons fish sauce
2 tablespoons mild sweet
  chilli sauce
1 teaspoon cornflour
1/2 cup (125ml) chicken stock
2 tablespoons finely chopped
  fresh coriander leaves
2 tablespoons finely chopped
  fresh mint leaves
4 green onions, sliced thickly

1 Cook noodles in large saucepan of boiling water, uncovered, until just tender; drain.

2 Heat oil in wok or large frying pan; swirl egg around base of wok to form a thin omelette. Cook until set; remove from wok. Roll omelette firmly; cut into thin slices.

3 Heat extra oil in wok; stir-fry combined pork, ginger and garlic until pork is cooked.

4 Add sauces and blended cornflour and stock; stir until mixture boils and thickens slightly.

5 Add noodles, omelette strips, herbs and onion; stir until hot.

SERVES 4

per serving 17.7g fat; 2155kJ

hoisin pork with green beans

PREPARATION TIME 15 MINUTES (plus marinating time) • COOKING TIME 15 MINUTES

500g pork fillets, sliced thinly
1 small fresh red chilli,
chopped finely
1 teaspoon grated fresh ginger
1 clove garlic, crushed
1 teaspoon sesame oil
2 tablespoons hoisin sauce
1 tablespoon peanut oil
1 small leek (200g),
chopped coarsely
250g green beans, sliced thickly
2 teaspoons fish sauce
1 teaspoon cornflour
1/2 cup (125ml) chicken stock

1 Combine pork, chilli, ginger, garlic, sesame oil and hoisin sauce in medium bowl. Cover; refrigerate 3 hours or overnight.

2 Heat half of the peanut oil in wok or large frying pan. Stir-fry undrained pork mixture, in batches, until pork is browned; remove from wok.

3 Heat remaining peanut oil in wok; stir-fry leek and beans.

4 Return pork mixture to wok. Add fish sauce and blended cornflour and stock; stir until sauce boils and thickens slightly.

SERVES 4

per serving 9.5g fat; 991kJ

pork with chinese cabbage and noodles

PREPARATION TIME 20 MINUTES • COOKING TIME 25 MINUTES

375g fresh egg noodles
1 tablespoon peanut oil
1 clove garlic, crushed
2 teaspoons finely chopped fresh lemon grass
$1/2$ teaspoon five spice powder
400g pork fillets, sliced thinly
1 medium red capsicum (200g), sliced thinly
5 green onions, chopped coarsely
$1/4$ medium chinese cabbage (200g), shredded
2 tablespoons oyster sauce
1 tablespoon soy sauce
2 tablespoons mild sweet chilli sauce
2 teaspoons sesame oil
$1/2$ teaspoon cornflour
$2/3$ cup (160ml) chicken stock

1 Cook noodles in large saucepan of boiling water, uncovered, until just tender; drain.

2 Heat half of the peanut oil in wok or large frying pan; stir-fry garlic, lemon grass and spice powder until fragrant.

3 Add pork, in batches. Stir-fry until pork is browned; remove from wok.

4 Heat remaining peanut oil in wok; stir-fry capsicum, onion and cabbage until cabbage is just wilted.

5 Return pork to wok. Add sauces, sesame oil and cornflour blended with stock; stir until mixture boils and thickens slightly.

6 Serve pork on noodles.

SERVES 4

per serving 11.2g fat; 1956kJ

thai fried noodles with pork and peanuts

PREPARATION TIME 10 MINUTES • COOKING TIME 20 MINUTES

500g hokkien noodles
2 teaspoons thai red curry paste
400g pork fillets, sliced thinly
1 tablespoon peanut oil
1 tablespoon soy sauce
2 teaspoons fish sauce
2 teaspoons cornflour
1/2 cup (125ml) chicken stock
1/3 cup (50g) unsalted
   roasted peanuts
2 tablespoons finely chopped
   fresh coriander leaves

1 Rinse noodles under hot water; drain. Transfer noodles to large bowl; separate with fork.

2 Combine curry paste and pork.

3 Heat half of the oil in wok or large frying pan. Stir-fry pork mixture, in batches, until pork is browned; remove from wok.

4 Heat remaining oil in wok. Stir-fry noodles until hot.

5 Add sauces and blended cornflour and stock; stir until mixture boils and thickens slightly.

6 Return pork to wok. Add peanuts and coriander; stir until hot.

SERVES 4

per serving 14.1g fat; 1621kJ

pork with mushrooms, ginger and bok choy

PREPARATION TIME 10 MINUTES (plus soaking time) • COOKING TIME 20 MINUTES

15g dried shiitake mushrooms
1 tablespoon peanut oil
3 teaspoons grated fresh ginger
450g pork fillets, sliced thinly
150g oyster mushrooms
150g button mushrooms, halved
1 tablespoon hoisin sauce
1 teaspoon cornflour
1/2 cup (125ml) chicken stock
250g bok choy, chopped roughly

1 Soak mushrooms in boiling water 20 minutes; drain. Discard stems; slice caps.

2 Heat oil in wok or large frying pan; stir-fry ginger until fragrant.

3 Add pork, in batches. Stir-fry until pork is browned; remove from wok.

4 Stir-fry mushrooms until hot.

5 Return pork to wok. Add sauce and blended cornflour and stock; stir until sauce boils and thickens slightly.

6 Add bok choy; stir-fry until just wilted.

SERVES 4

per serving 7.9g fat; 846kJ

pork and macadamia stir-fried salad

PREPARATION TIME 20 MINUTES (plus marinating time) • COOKING TIME 25 MINUTES

500g pork fillets, sliced thinly
2 tablespoons teriyaki sauce
1 teaspoon grated orange rind
1 clove garlic, crushed
1 teaspoon cracked
   black peppercorns
1 tablespoon light olive oil
1 small kumara (250g),
   sliced thinly
1/4 cup (35g) macadamias
200g swiss brown
   mushrooms, halved
4 green onions, chopped coarsely
2 tablespoons cider vinegar
1/3 cup (80ml) light olive oil, extra
1/4 teaspoon sugar
120g rocket
1/4 cup small fresh basil leaves

1 Combine pork, sauce, rind, garlic and peppercorns in medium bowl.
   Cover; refrigerate 3 hours or overnight.

2 Heat half of the oil in wok or large frying pan. Stir-fry kumara until just
   tender; remove from wok.

3 Stir-fry nuts until browned lightly; remove from wok.

4 Heat remaining oil in wok. Stir-fry pork mixture, in batches, until
   browned; remove from wok.

5 Stir-fry mushrooms and onion until mushrooms are softened slightly.

6 Return kumara and pork mixture to wok. Add vinegar, extra oil and
   sugar; stir until sauce boils. Add rocket and basil.

7 Serve sprinkled with nuts.

SERVES 4

per serving 32.9g fat; 2013kJ

orange pork with soy thyme sauce

PREPARATION TIME 15 MINUTES (plus marinating time) • COOKING TIME 20 MINUTES

500g pork fillets, sliced thinly
1 medium white onion (150g),
  sliced thinly
3/4 cup (180ml) orange juice
2 tablespoons soy sauce
1 tablespoon finely chopped
  fresh thyme
2 cloves garlic, crushed
1 tablespoon peanut oil
1/3 cup (70g) water chestnuts,
  sliced thickly
1 tablespoon marmalade
2 teaspoons cornflour
500g english spinach
11/2 cups (120g) bean sprouts

1 Combine pork, onion, juice, sauce, thyme and garlic in medium bowl. Cover; refrigerate 3 hours or overnight.

2 Drain pork; reserve marinade.

3 Heat oil in wok or large frying pan. Stir-fry pork, in batches, until browned; remove from wok.

4 Place chestnuts and marmalade in wok with cornflour blended with reserved marinade; stir until mixture boils and thickens slightly.

5 Return pork to wok. Add spinach and sprouts; stir until spinach is just wilted.

SERVES 4

per serving 7.9g fat; 1068kJ

sherried hoisin pork with lemon

PREPARATION TIME 25 MINUTES (plus marinating time)
COOKING TIME 20 MINUTES

400g pork fillets, sliced thinly
1/3 cup (80ml) hoisin sauce
2 tablespoons dry sherry
2 teaspoons sesame oil
1 clove garlic, crushed
2 medium carrots (240g)
1 tablespoon peanut oil
5 slices lemon
300g sugar snap peas
2 cups bean sprouts (160g)

1 Combine pork, sauce, sherry, sesame oil and garlic in medium bowl. Cover; refrigerate 3 hours or overnight.

2 Drain pork; reserve marinade.

3 Using vegetable peeler, cut carrots into long thin strips.

4 Heat half of the peanut oil in wok or large frying pan. Stir-fry lemon until browned; remove from wok.

5 Stir-fry carrot and peas; remove from wok.

6 Heat remaining peanut oil in wok; stir-fry pork, in batches, until pork is browned.

7 Return pork, lemon slices, carrot and peas to wok. Add sprouts and reserved marinade; stir until sauce boils.

SERVES 4

per serving 10.6g fat; 1155kJ

crispy prosciutto with tomatoes and spaghetti

PREPARATION TIME 15 MINUTES • COOKING TIME 25 MINUTES

350g spaghetti
2 tablespoons shredded fresh
basil leaves
2 tablespoons finely chopped
fresh parsley
2 tablespoons olive oil
1 tablespoon lemon juice
1 tablespoon balsamic vinegar
2 teaspoons olive oil, extra
6 slices prosciutto (90g),
chopped roughly
2 cloves garlic, crushed
8 medium egg tomatoes
(600g), quartered
¼ cup (40g) pine nuts, toasted

1 Cook spaghetti, uncovered, in large saucepan of boiling water until just tender; drain.

2 Meanwhile, combine basil, parsley, oil, juice and vinegar in screw-top jar; shake well.

3 Heat extra oil in wok or large frying pan. Stir-fry prosciutto and garlic until prosciutto is crisp; drain on absorbent paper.

4 Stir-fry tomato until just soft.

5 Add spaghetti, prosciutto, basil mixture and nuts; stir-fry until hot.

SERVES 4

per serving 21.2g fat; 2214kJ

mustard pork with olives and artichokes

PREPARATION TIME 20 MINUTES (plus marinating time) • COOKING TIME 15 MINUTES

500g pork fillets, sliced thinly
2 tablespoons red wine vinegar
2 tablespoons dijon mustard
1 tablespoon soy sauce
1 clove garlic, crushed
2 teaspoons sugar
2 tablespoons olive oil
2 medium red onions (340g),
  sliced thinly
500g english spinach,
  chopped roughly
400g can artichoke hearts,
  drained, halved
1/2 cup (75g) drained sun-dried
  tomatoes, halved
1/2 cup (60g) seeded black olives

1 Combine pork, vinegar, mustard, sauce, garlic and sugar in medium bowl. Cover; refrigerate 3 hours or overnight.

2 Heat half of the oil in wok or large frying pan. Stir-fry pork mixture, in batches, until pork is browned; remove from wok.

3 Heat remaining oil in wok; stir-fry onion until just soft.

4 Return pork mixture to wok with spinach, artichoke, tomato and olives; stir-fry until spinach is just wilted.

SERVES 4

per serving 14g fat; 1317kJ

barbecued pork chow mein

PREPARATION TIME 25 MINUTES • COOKING TIME 25 MINUTES

375g thin fresh egg noodles
2 tablespoons peanut oil
2 teaspoons sesame oil
250g chinese barbecued pork,
  sliced thinly
1 tablespoon soy sauce
2 tablespoons oyster sauce
1/4 cup (60ml) plum sauce
3 teaspoons cornflour
3/4 cup (180ml) chicken stock
1/4 medium chinese cabbage
  (200g), shredded
2 green onions, sliced thickly

1 Cook noodles in large saucepan of boiling water, uncovered, until just tender; drain.

2 Heat oils in wok or large frying pan. Shape noodles into 25cm round; cook, without stirring, until browned and crisp underneath, pressing down throughout cooking.

3 Slide noodles onto an oven tray; invert into wok with cooked side up. Cook until crisp underneath. Remove from wok; keep warm.

4 Combine pork, sauces and cornflour blended with stock; stir until mixture boils and thickens slightly.

5 Add cabbage; stir until cabbage is just wilted.

6 Serve pork mixture on noodles, topped with onion.

SERVES 4

per serving 15.1g fat; 2132kJ

chinese pork sausages with mushrooms and noodles

PREPARATION TIME 20 MINUTES • COOKING TIME 20 MINUTES

375g thin fresh egg noodles
1 tablespoon peanut oil
1 medium brown onion (150g),
  sliced thinly
2 cloves garlic, crushed
1 teaspoon grated fresh ginger
250g button mushrooms,
  sliced thinly
3 chinese pork sausages (95g),
  sliced thinly
1 small red capsicum (150g),
  sliced thinly
250g english spinach,
  chopped coarsely
2 tablespoons oyster sauce
1 tablespoon mild sweet
  chilli sauce
2 tablespoons salt-reduced
  soy sauce
2 teaspoons cornflour
1/2 cup (125ml) chicken stock

1 Cook noodles in large saucepan
  of boiling water, uncovered,
  until just tender; drain.

2 Heat oil in wok or large frying
  pan; stir-fry onion, garlic,
  ginger, mushrooms, sausage and
  capsicum until mushrooms
  are soft.

3 Add spinach, sauces and
  cornflour blended with stock;
  stir until spinach has wilted.

4 Add noodles; stir until hot.

SERVES 4

per serving 11.6g fat; 1726kJ

chilli pork with oyster sauce

PREPARATION TIME 15 MINUTES • COOKING TIME 10 MINUTES

1 tablespoon peanut oil
450g pork fillets, sliced thinly
1 clove garlic, crushed
1 medium white onion (150g), sliced thinly
1 large red capsicum (350g), sliced thinly
1 small green zucchini (90g), sliced thinly
1 small yellow zucchini (90g), sliced thinly
1/4 cup (60ml) oyster sauce
1 tablespoon mild sweet chilli sauce
1 tablespoon coarsely chopped fresh coriander leaves

1 Heat oil in wok or large frying pan. Stir-fry pork, in batches, until browned; remove from wok.

2 Stir-fry garlic and onion until onion is just soft.

3 Add capsicum and zucchini; stir-fry.

4 Return pork to wok. Add sauces; stir-fry until hot. Serve sprinkled with coriander.

SERVES 4

per serving 7.6g fat; 907kJ

seafood

Seafood is the ideal food for stir-frying as it needs only quick cooking to give perfect, tender results. Over-cooking, or reheating, will toughen all seafood. Here, we combine seafood with some exciting new ingredients and some favourite, familiar ones. Mouth-watering combinations include tuna with basil, capsicum and rocket, and sweet chilli noodles with clams and mussels.

crispy tuna with mint and chilli

PREPARATION TIME 25 MINUTES • COOKING TIME 20 MINUTES

650g tuna steaks
2 tablespoons cornflour
1/2 teaspoon sichuan pepper
2 tablespoons vegetable oil
1 medium white onion (150g), sliced thinly
1 medium red capsicum (200g), sliced thinly
1 medium yellow capsicum (200g), sliced thinly
1 tablespoon soy sauce
1 tablespoon mild sweet chilli sauce
1 tablespoon sake
1 tablespoon lime juice
2 teaspoons honey
1 cup (60g) firmly packed snow pea sprouts

1 Remove skin from tuna. Cut tuna into 3cm pieces; pat dry with absorbent paper.

2 Toss tuna gently in combined cornflour and pepper; shake away excess flour mixture.

3 Heat oil in wok or large frying pan. Stir-fry tuna, in batches, until tuna is cooked as desired; remove from wok. Drain on absorbent paper.

4 Stir-fry onion and capsicums until onion is just soft.

5 Add sauces, sake, juice and honey; stir until hot.

6 Serve tuna over vegetable mixture and sprouts.

SERVES 4

per serving 18.9g fat; 1769kJ

cajun-style fish salad

PREPARATION TIME 15 MINUTES • COOKING TIME 15 MINUTES

400g boneless white fish fillets
1 teaspoon dried thyme leaves
1 teaspoon dried parsley flakes
2 teaspoons garlic salt
1 teaspoon paprika
1 teaspoon onion powder
1/2 teaspoon cracked black peppercorns
300g baby yellow squash, sliced thinly
150g green beans, sliced thickly
1 tablespoon vegetable oil
30g butter
few drops Tabasco sauce

1 Cut fish into 3cm pieces; pat dry with absorbent paper.

2 Add fish to combined herbs and spices; mix well.

3 Add squash and beans to large saucepan of boiling water; drain immediately. Rinse under cold water; drain well.

4 Heat oil in wok or large frying pan. Stir-fry fish, in batches, until tender; return fish to wok.

5 Add squash, beans and butter; stir-fry until hot.

6 Add sauce to taste.

SERVES 4

per serving 13.5g fat; 975kJ

sweet chilli noodles with clams and mussels

PREPARATION TIME 15 MINUTES (plus soaking time) • COOKING TIME 15 MINUTES

1kg fresh clams
800g small black mussels
375g hokkien noodles
2 x 425g cans tomatoes
$1/3$ cup (80ml) mild sweet chilli sauce
$1/4$ cup (60ml) oyster sauce
1 tablespoon cornflour
2 tablespoons lime juice

1 Soak clams in cold water for 2 hours; change water twice during soaking.

2 Scrub mussels; remove beards.

3 Rinse noodles under hot water; drain. Transfer noodles to large bowl; separate with fork.

4 Heat undrained crushed tomatoes, sauces and noodles in wok or large frying pan.

5 Add clams, mussels, and blended cornflour and juice; stir until mixture boils and thickens.

6 Reduce heat. Cover; cook few minutes or until clams and mussels open.

SERVES 4

per serving 3.2g fat; 1641kJ

coconut ginger carrots and prawns

PREPARATION TIME 25 MINUTES • COOKING TIME 20 MINUTES

800g medium uncooked prawns
3 cloves garlic, crushed
1 small brown onion (80g),
 chopped roughly
2 teaspoons grated fresh ginger
1/2 teaspoon ground turmeric
2 teaspoons mild curry powder
8 cardamom seeds
1 teaspoon cumin seeds
2 tablespoons vegetable oil
2 large carrots (360g),
 grated coarsely
4 green onions, sliced thinly
400ml coconut milk

1 Shell and devein prawns, leaving tails intact.

2 Process garlic, brown onion, ginger, turmeric, curry powder, seeds and half of the oil until smooth.

3 Heat remaining oil in wok or large frying pan. Stir-fry garlic mixture until fragrant.

4 Add carrot; stir-fry 2 minutes. Remove from wok.

5 Stir-fry combined prawns and green onion, in batches, until prawns are just tender. Return prawns and onion to wok with carrots and coconut milk; stir until hot.

SERVES 4

per serving 31.2g fat; 1754kJ

scallops and snow peas with noodles

PREPARATION TIME 15 MINUTES • COOKING TIME 15 MINUTES

1/3 cup (75g) sugar
1/3 cup (80ml) water
1/2 cup (125ml) lime juice
2 tablespoons oyster sauce
1 clove garlic, crushed
250g thin fresh egg noodles
1 tablespoon peanut oil
1/2 teaspoon sesame oil
600g scallops
1 medium carrot (120g), cut into thin strips
8 green onions, sliced thinly
150g snow peas
2 tablespoons finely chopped fresh coriander leaves

1 Combine sugar, the water and juice in small saucepan. Cook, stirring, without boiling, until sugar is dissolved; bring to a boil. Boil, uncovered, 3 minutes; stir in sauce and garlic.

2 Cook noodles in large saucepan of boiling water, uncovered, until just tender; drain.

3 Heat oils in wok or large frying pan. Stir-fry scallops, in batches, until just tender; remove from wok.

4 Stir-fry carrot, onion and peas.

5 Return scallops to wok. Add lime mixture; stir until hot.

6 Serve scallop mixture over noodles, sprinkled with coriander.

SERVES 4

per serving 7.1g fat; 1372kJ

tuna with basil, capsicum and rocket

PREPARATION TIME 20 MINUTES (plus marinating time) • COOKING TIME 20 MINUTES

1kg fresh tuna
1 tablespoon olive oil
1 tablespoon lemon juice
1 tablespoon finely chopped
   fresh oregano leaves
1 clove garlic, crushed
2 tablespoons pine nuts
2 medium brown onions (300g),
   sliced thinly
3 medium zucchini (360g),
   sliced thinly
1 large red capsicum (350g),
   sliced thinly
1/4 cup (60ml) lemon juice, extra
1/2 cup (125ml) olive oil, extra
1 clove garlic, crushed, extra
pinch sugar
1/2 teaspoon cracked
   black peppercorns
2 teaspoons salt-reduced soy sauce
2 tablespoons finely chopped
   fresh basil leaves
120g rocket

1 Remove skin from tuna; cut tuna into 3cm pieces.

2 Combine tuna, half of the oil, juice, oregano and garlic in medium bowl. Cover; refrigerate 3 hours or overnight.

3 Heat half of the remaining oil in wok or large frying pan. Stir-fry pine nuts until browned; remove from wok.

4 Heat remaining oil in wok. Stir-fry tuna mixture, in batches, until tuna is just tender; remove from wok.

5 Stir-fry onion, zucchini and capsicum.

6 Return tuna mixture to wok with extra juice, extra oil, extra garlic, sugar, peppercorns, sauce, basil and rocket; stir until sauce boils.

7 Serve sprinkled with pine nuts.

SERVES 4

per serving 55g fat; 3400kJ

spicy calamari stir-fry

PREPARATION TIME 20 MINUTES • COOKING TIME 15 MINUTES

600g calamari tubes
2 tablespoons vegetable oil
1 small leek (200g), sliced thickly
1 medium red capsicum (200g),
  sliced thickly
1 tablespoon oyster sauce
1 tablespoon barbecue sauce
2 teaspoons mild sweet
  chilli sauce
1 teaspoon cornflour
1/2 cup (125ml) chicken stock

1 Score inside surface of calamari; cut calamari into 4cm squares.

2 Heat half of the oil in wok or large frying pan. Stir-fry calamari, in batches, until just tender; remove from wok.

3 Heat remaining oil in wok; stir-fry leek and capsicum until leek is soft.

4 Return calamari to wok; Add sauces and blended cornflour and stock; stir until sauce boils and thickens slightly.

SERVES 4

per serving 11.4g fat; 1005kJ

chilli calamari
stir-fried salad

PREPARATION TIME 10 MINUTES • COOKING TIME 10 MINUTES

4 medium calamari tubes (800g)
2 tablespoons olive oil
2 cloves garlic, crushed
$^1/_2$ teaspoon sambal oelek
$^1/_2$ teaspoon ground black peppercorns
1 tablespoon balsamic vinegar
2 teaspoons white wine vinegar
1 teaspoon sugar
mixed salad leaves

1 Score inside surface of calamari; cut calamari into 6cm pieces.

2 Heat half of the oil in wok or large frying pan. Stir-fry combined calamari, garlic, sambal oelek and peppercorns, in batches, until calamari is just tender; return calamari to wok.

3 Add remaining oil, combined vinegars and sugar; stir until hot.

4 Serve with mixed salad leaves.

SERVES 4

per serving 11.6g fat; 1037kJ

mediterranean octopus stir-fry

PREPARATION TIME 25 MINUTES (plus refrigeration time) • COOKING TIME 25 MINUTES

1kg baby octopus
1/4 cup (60ml) dry red wine
1/4 cup (60ml) lemon juice
2 tablespoons brown sugar
2 cloves garlic, crushed
2 tablespoons finely chopped
 fresh oregano leaves
2 bay leaves
2 tablespoons olive oil
2 medium white onions (300g),
 sliced thinly
1 large yellow capsicum (350g),
 chopped coarsely
2 large tomatoes (500g), seeded,
 sliced thickly
1/2 cup (60g) seeded black olives
1 tablespoon tomato paste
2 teaspoons cornflour
1/4 cup (60ml) water
1/4 cup shredded fresh basil leaves

1 Remove and discard heads and beaks from octopus; cut octopus into quarters.

2 Combine octopus, wine, juice, sugar, garlic, oregano and bay leaves in large bowl. Cover; refrigerate 3 hours or overnight.

3 Heat half of the oil in wok or large frying pan. Stir-fry octopus mixture, in batches, until just tender; remove from wok.

4 Heat remaining oil in wok; stir-fry onion and capsicum until onion is just soft.

5 Add tomato; stir-fry.

6 Return octopus mixture to wok with olives, paste and blended cornflour and water; stir until sauce boils and thickens slightly.

7 Discard bay leaves; stir in basil.

SERVES 4

per serving 11.1g fat; 1340kJ

quick prawn curry with coriander

PREPARATION TIME 15 MINUTES • COOKING TIME 15 MINUTES

500g medium uncooked prawns
1 tablespoon peanut oil
1 clove garlic, crushed
2 teaspoons curry powder
4 green onions, chopped finely
1 medium red capsicum (200g),
  sliced thinly
3 trimmed sticks celery (225g),
  sliced thinly
³/4 cup (180ml) cream
1 tablespoon golden syrup
¹/4 teaspoon sesame oil
1 tablespoon finely chopped
  fresh coriander leaves

1 Shell and devein prawns, leaving tails intact.

2 Heat peanut oil in wok or large frying pan. Stir-fry garlic and curry powder until fragrant.

3 Add prawns, onion, capsicum and celery; stir-fry until prawns are just tender.

4 Add combined cream, golden syrup and sesame oil; stir until hot.

5 Serve sprinkled with coriander.

SERVES 4

per serving 25.2g fat; 1346kJ

quick fish and prawn curry

PREPARATION TIME 25 MINUTES • COOKING TIME 20 MINUTES

$1/2$ **teaspoon grated lemon rind**
$1/3$ **cup (80ml) lemon juice**
1 tablespoon grated fresh ginger
2 cloves garlic, peeled
1 teaspoon sambal oelek
2 teaspoons fish sauce
2 teaspoons mild curry powder
$1/4$ **cup (35g) unsalted roasted peanuts**
500g medium uncooked prawns
2 tablespoons peanut oil
800g boneless white fish fillets, chopped roughly
3 green onions, sliced thinly
2 teaspoons cornflour
$1/4$ **cup (60ml) water**

1 Blend or process rind, juice, ginger, garlic, sambal oelek, sauce, curry powder and peanuts until smooth.

2 Shell and devein prawns, leaving heads and tails intact.

3 Heat oil in wok or large frying pan. Stir-fry prawns and fish, separately, in batches, until prawns and fish are just tender; remove from wok.

4 Add onion to wok; stir-fry.

5 Return prawns and fish to wok. Add curry mixture and blended cornflour and water; stir until sauce boils and thickens.

SERVES 4

per serving 18.8g fat; 1730kJ

vegetarian

Vegetables mix and match brilliantly with all kinds of ingredients to produce quick and creative meals and accompaniments. Tastes and textures really triumph in this section with surprises such as honey, corn and water chestnuts, and snow pea and almond stir-fry.

tofu and vegetable stir-fry

PREPARATION TIME 25 MINUTES • COOKING TIME 20 MINUTES

350g cauliflower, chopped coarsely
350g broccoli, chopped coarsely
250g asparagus, sliced thickly
350g green beans, sliced thickly
3 medium carrots (360g), sliced thinly
1/4 cup (60ml) olive oil
2 cloves garlic, crushed
1 tablespoon finely chopped fresh thyme
1 teaspoon cracked black peppercorns
375g packet firm tofu, cubed
2 medium brown onions (300g), sliced thickly
250g button mushrooms, sliced thickly
1/2 cup (125ml) white wine
3 teaspoons cornflour
1 cup (250ml) vegetable stock

1 Add cauliflower, broccoli, asparagus, beans and carrot to large saucepan of boiling water. Boil, uncovered, 2 minutes; drain.

2 Heat oil in wok or large frying pan. Stir-fry garlic, thyme, peppercorns and tofu until tofu is browned lightly; remove from wok.

3 Stir-fry onion and mushroom until onion is just soft.

4 Add vegetable mixture, wine and blended cornflour and stock; stir until sauce boils and thickens slightly.

5 Return tofu to wok.

SERVES 6

per serving 14.1g fat; 1051kJ

indian-style vegetables

PREPARATION TIME 15 MINUTES • COOKING TIME 15 MINUTES

1 tablespoon peanut oil
1 clove garlic, crushed
1 teaspoon ground cumin
1 teaspoon ground caraway
1 teaspoon ground nutmeg
1 teaspoon mild curry powder
1/2 teaspoon ground turmeric
1 medium white onion (150g),
　sliced thickly
1 medium carrot (120g),
　sliced thinly
300g yellow squash, quartered
1 medium green capsicum (200g),
　sliced thickly
200g button mushrooms, halved
1 teaspoon cornflour
3/4 cup (180ml) coconut cream
1 tablespoon finely chopped fresh
　coriander leaves

1 Heat oil in wok or large frying
　pan; stir-fry garlic and spices
　until fragrant.

2 Add onion and carrot; stir-fry
　until onion is soft.

3 Add squash, capsicum and
　mushrooms; stir-fry.

4 Add blended cornflour and
　coconut cream; stir until mixture
　boils and thickens slightly.

5 Serve sprinkled with coriander.

SERVES 4 AS AN ACCOMPANIMENT

per serving 14.7g fat; 842kJ

thai noodles with coriander

PREPARATION TIME 10 MINUTES • COOKING TIME 10 MINUTES

375g thin fresh egg noodles
1 tablespoon peanut oil
2 cloves garlic, crushed
2 tablespoons lime juice
2 tablespoons light soy sauce
1/2 teaspoon dried crushed chillies
2 cups bean sprouts (160g)
1/2 cup (75g) unsalted
  roasted peanuts
2 tablespoons finely chopped
  fresh coriander leaves

1 Cook noodles in large saucepan of boiling water, uncovered, until just tender; drain.

2 Heat oil in wok or large frying pan; stir-fry garlic until it just changes colour.

3 Add noodles, juice, sauce, chilli, sprouts and peanuts; stir-fry until hot.

4 Stir in coriander.

SERVES 4 AS AN ACCOMPANIMENT

per serving 15.6g fat; 1742kJ

stir-fried greens with green beans

PREPARATION TIME 10 MINUTES • COOKING TIME 10 MINUTES

350g green beans, halved
2 tablespoons peanut oil
1 teaspoon sesame oil
2 cloves garlic, crushed
2 teaspoons grated fresh ginger
8 green onions, chopped roughly
500g english spinach, chopped coarsely
670g baby bok choy, chopped coarsely
1 tablespoon teriyaki sauce
1 tablespoon salt-reduced soy sauce
1 tablespoon mild sweet chilli sauce
2 tablespoons finely chopped fresh coriander leaves

1 Add beans to large saucepan of boiling water; drain.

2 Heat oils in wok or large frying pan; stir-fry garlic, ginger and onion until onion is soft.

3 Add beans, spinach and bok choy; stir-fry until bok choy is just wilted.

4 Add sauces; stir until hot.

5 Serve sprinkled with coriander.

SERVES 4 AS AN ACCOMPANIMENT

per serving 11.2g fat; 658kJ

eggplants with beans and mushrooms

PREPARATION TIME 10 MINUTES (plus standing time) • COOKING TIME 20 MINUTES

3 medium eggplants (900g),
  chopped roughly
coarse cooking salt
300g frozen broad beans
1/3 cup (80ml) olive oil
1 medium red onion (170g),
  sliced thinly
1 clove garlic, crushed
200g button mushrooms, halved
200g cup mushrooms, sliced thickly
3/4 cup (180ml) tomato puree
1/4 cup (60ml) dry white wine
1 tablespoon coarsely chopped
  fresh oregano leaves

1 Sprinkle eggplant with salt. Stand 20 minutes; rinse. Drain; pat dry with absorbent paper.

2 Boil, steam or microwave beans until tender; drain. Remove skins from beans.

3 Heat half the oil in wok or large frying pan. Stir-fry eggplant, in batches, until tender; remove from wok.

4 Heat remaining oil in wok; stir-fry onion, garlic and mushrooms until mushrooms are tender.

5 Return eggplant to wok. Add beans, puree, wine and oregano; stir until hot.

SERVES 4

per serving 19.5g fat; 1218kJ

honey, corn and water chestnuts

PREPARATION TIME 10 MINUTES • COOKING TIME 10 MINUTES

1 tablespoon peanut oil
1 clove garlic, crushed
1 medium white onion (150g),
  chopped coarsely
1 large carrot (180g),
  sliced thinly
2 trimmed sticks celery (150g),
  sliced thinly
1 large red capsicum (350g),
  sliced thinly
100g green beans
300g broccoli, chopped coarsely
2 x 230g can water
  chestnuts, drained
425g can baby corn, drained
1¹/₂ tablespoons honey
1 teaspoon cornflour
2 tablespoons teriyaki sauce
1 teaspoon mild sweet chilli sauce

1 Heat oil in wok or large frying pan; stir-fry garlic, onion and carrot until onion is soft.

2 Add celery, capsicum, beans and broccoli; stir-fry.

3 Add chestnuts, corn, honey and blended cornflour and sauces; stir until sauce boils and thickens slightly.

SERVES 4 AS AN ACCOMPANIMENT

per serving 6.6g fat; 1014kJ

snow pea and almond stir-fry

PREPARATION TIME 10 MINUTES • COOKING TIME 10 MINUTES

500g hokkien noodles
1 tablespoon peanut oil
1 clove garlic, crushed
1 medium white onion (150g), sliced thinly
200g snow peas
2 tablespoons plum sauce
2 teaspoons soy sauce
1/2 teaspoon cornflour
1/2 teaspoon sugar
1/2 cup (125ml) vegetable stock
1/2 cup (80g) blanched almonds, toasted

1 Rinse noodles under hot water; drain. Transfer noodles to large bowl; separate with fork.

2 Heat oil in wok or large frying pan; stir-fry garlic and onion until onion is soft.

3 Add snow peas; stir-fry.

4 Add noodles, sauces and blended cornflour, sugar and stock; stir until mixture boils and thickens slightly.

5 Stir in nuts.

SERVES 6 AS AN ACCOMPANIMENT

per serving 17.3g fat; 2259kJ

lentil balls with tomatoes and rocket

PREPARATION TIME 30 MINUTES • COOKING TIME 25 MINUTES

1 cup (200g) red lentils
2 tablespoons olive oil
2 medium zucchini (240g), grated coarsely
1 small brown onion (80g), chopped finely
1 small fresh red chilli, chopped finely
1 cup (70g) stale breadcrumbs
1/4 cup (35g) white sesame seeds, toasted
1 tablespoon finely chopped fresh coriander leaves
1/3 cup (35g) packaged breadcrumbs
vegetable oil for deep-frying
5 medium egg tomatoes (375g), quartered
2 cloves garlic, crushed
120g rocket
2 tablespoons shredded fresh mint
2 tablespoons shredded fresh basil
1/4 cup (60ml) white wine vinegar

1 Add lentils to large saucepan of boiling water; boil, uncovered, about 8 minutes or until just tender. Drain; press out liquid.

2 Meanwhile, heat half of the olive oil in wok or large frying pan; stir-fry zucchini, onion and chilli until onion is just soft.

3 Combine lentils, zucchini mixture, stale breadcrumbs, seeds and coriander in medium bowl. Roll rounded teaspoons of mixture into balls; toss in packaged breadcrumbs.

4 Deep-fry balls, in batches, in hot vegetable oil until browned; drain on absorbent paper.

5 Heat remaining olive oil in wok; stir-fry tomatoes and garlic.

6 Return lentil balls to wok; stir until hot.

7 Remove wok from heat; add rocket, mint, basil and vinegar.

SERVES 4

per serving 16.5g fat; 1924kJ

glossary

bacon rashers bacon slices.

barbecue sauce a spicy sauce available from supermarkets, consisting of apples, tomatoes, sugar, molasses, vinegar, spices and onion.

bean sprouts also known as bean shoots; we used soy bean sprouts.

beans

GREEN sometimes called french beans.

SNAKE long (about 40cm), thin, round green beans; Asian in origin.

beef

EYE FILLET tenderloin.

MINCED ground beef.

RIB-EYE ROLL AND STEAK (SCOTCH FILLET) the section of eye muscle which runs through the forequarter.

RUMP STEAK boneless piece of meat that covers the hip bone.

belacan dried shrimp paste sold in slabs or flat cakes.

black bean sauce made from fermented soy beans, water and wheat flour.

bok choy also called pak choi or chinese white cabbage; has a mild mustard taste and is good braised or stir-fried. Baby bok choy is also available.

burghul (cracked wheat) wheat that is steamed until partly cooked, then dried and cracked.

cabanossi a ready-to-eat sausage; also known as cabana.

caperberries fruit formed after the caper buds have flowered; caperberries are pickled.

capers pickled buds of a Mediterranean shrub.

capsicum also known as peppers or bell peppers; seeds and membranes should be discarded before use.

chicken tenderloin the thin strip of meat lying just under the breast.

chickpeas also known as garbanzos.

chillies are available in many different types and sizes. Use rubber gloves when chopping fresh chillies as they can burn your skin.

chinese barbecued pork roasted pork fillets available from many Asian food and specialty stores.

chinese sausages highly spiced, bright red, thin pork sausages. Because of the high spice content, the meat is preserved and can be kept at room temperature.

chipolatas tiny sausages.

choy sum also known as flowering bok choy or flowering white cabbage.

coriander also known as cilantro or chinese parsley; bright-green-leafed herb with a pungent flavour. Often stirred into a dish just before serving for maximum impact.

GROUND ground dried coriander seeds, sold in supermarkets.

cornflour also known as cornstarch; used as a thickening agent in cooking.

couscous a fine cereal made from semolina.

cream, sour a thick, commercially cultured, soured cream with 35 per cent fat content.

curly endive also known as frisee; a curly-leafed green vegetable.

curry paste we used bottled curry pastes; available from supermarkets and Asian specialty stores.

GREEN consisting of red onion, green chilli, soy bean oil, garlic, galangal, lemon grass, shrimp paste, citrus peel, salt, coriander seed and citric acid.

MADRAS consisting of coriander, cumin, pepper, turmeric, chilli, garlic, ginger, vinegar and oil.

RED consisting of chilli, onion, garlic, oil, lemon rind, shrimp paste, cumin, paprika, turmeric and pepper.

TANDOORI consisting of garlic, tamarind, ginger, coriander, chilli and spices.

THAI RED consisting of red onion, red chilli, soy bean oil, garlic, galangal, lemon grass, shrimp paste, citrus peel, salt, coriander seed and citric acid.

TIKKA consisting of chilli, coriander, cumin, lentil flour, garlic, ginger, oil, turmeric, fennel, pepper, cloves, cinnamon and cardamom.

VINDALOO a fiery hot/sour flavour consisting of coriander, cumin, turmeric, chilli, ginger, garlic, tamarind, lentil flour and spices.

curry powder consisting of chilli, coriander, cumin, fennel, fenugreek and turmeric.

daikon radish a long white horseradish with a wonderful, sweet flavour.

eggplant also known as aubergine.

english spinach delicate, crinkled green leaves on thin stems; high in iron, it's good eaten raw in salads or added to stir-fries just before serving.

fish sauce made from the liquid drained from salted, fermented anchovies. It has a strong smell and taste; use sparingly.

five spice powder a pungent mixture of ground spices including cinnamon, cloves, fennel, star anise and sichuan peppers.

garam masala usually consisting of cardamom, cinnamon, cloves, coriander, cumin and nutmeg.

golden syrup made from sugar syrup, glucose, fructose and water. Maple, pancake syrup or honey can be substituted.

green ginger wine alcoholic ginger-flavoured sweet wine.

green peppercorns peppercorns preserved in brine.

hoisin sauce is a thick, sweet, Chinese barbecue sauce made from salted black beans, onions and garlic.

italian beef sausages large, fresh, highly seasoned sausages.

jam also known as preserve or conserve; most often made from fruit.

kumara orange-coloured sweet potato.

lamb

CUTLETS small, tender rib chops.

FILLETS tenderloin; the smaller piece of meat from a row of loin chops or cutlets.

TRIM LAMB boneless cuts; free of any external fat.

leek a member of the onion family, resembles the green onion but is much larger.

lettuce

COS also known as roma; has crisp, elongated leaves.

ICEBERG a heavy, firm, round lettuce with tightly packed leaves and crisp texture.

OAK LEAF also known as feville de chene. Available in both red and green leaf.

RADICCHIO a type of Italian lettuce with dark burgundy leaves.

lime leaves, kaffir available from many Asian food stores.

mirin sweet rice wine used in Japanese cooking.

mung beans also known as moong dal.

mushrooms

BUTTON small, cultivated white mushrooms having a delicate, subtle flavour.

ENOKI (ENOKITAKE) dainty, slender-stemmed mushrooms with tiny white to pale gold, rounded caps.

OYSTER (ABALONE) Grey-white mushrooms shaped like a fan.

SHIITAKE have a unique meaty flavour. Sold dried or fresh; soak dried mushrooms to rehydrate before use.

SHIMEJI Rarely more than 4cm in diameter, with a dimple in their concave caps, these light grey to fawn coloured mushrooms have a delicate texture and flavour.

SWISS BROWN light to dark brown mushrooms with full-bodied flavour. Button or cup mushrooms can be substituted.

mustard

DIJON a hot French mustard.

SEEDED prepared mustard containing crushed and whole mustard seeds.

SEEDS can be black or yellow.

noodles both fresh and dried are available; one can be substituted for the other, but cooking times will vary.

CELLOPHANE also known as bean thread or glass noodles. Thin and shiny; made from green mung bean flour.

EGG made from wheat flour, water and egg; strands vary in thickness.

FRIED also known as crispy or crunchy fried noodles.

FRESH RICE wide, almost white in colour; made from rice and vegetable oil. Must be covered with boiling water to remove starch and excess oil before use.

HOKKIEN also known as stir-fry noodles; fresh egg noodles resembling thick, yellow-brown spaghetti, needs no pre-cooking before use.

INSTANT also known as 2-minute noodles; small packages of quick-cooking noodles with flavour sachets.

RICE STICK a dried noodle, available flat and wide or very thin; made from rice flour and water.

RICE VERMICELLI also known as rice-flour noodles; made from ground rice, dried and best used either deep-fried or soaked, then tossed in a stir-fry or stirred into a soup.

SOBA Japanese dried noodles made of buckwheat flour.

oil

EXTRA VIRGIN the highest quality olive oil, obtained from the first pressing of the olives.

LIGHT OLIVE mild-tasting, light in flavour, colour and aroma, but not lower in kilojoules.

MACADAMIA oil extracted from macadamia nuts.

OLIVE a blend of refined and virgin olive oils.

PEANUT made from ground peanuts, this is the most commonly used oil in Asian cooking, a lighter vegetable type of oil can be substituted.

SESAME an oil made from roasted, crushed white sesame seeds, used for flavouring.

VEGETABLE we used a polyunsaturated vegetable oil.

WALNUT oil extracted from walnuts.

onion

GREEN also known as scallion or (incorrectly) shallot; an immature onion picked before the bulb has formed, having a long bright-green edible stalk.

POWDER dried ground onions.

RED also known as spanish, red spanish or bermuda onion; a sweet flavoured, large, purple-red onion.

SPRING has a crisp, narrow green-leafed top and a fairly large sweet white bulb.

oyster sauce a rich brown sauce made from oysters cooked in salt and soy sauce, then thickened with starches.

paprika both sweet and hot types are available.

plum sauce made from plums, sugar, chillies and spices.

pork

FILLET skinless, boneless eye-fillet cut from the loin.

LEG STRIPS strips cut from the pork leg.

SPARE RIBS cut from the pork belly.

prawns crustaceans also known as shrimp.

prosciutto salt-cured, air-dried (unsmoked), pressed ham.

red salsa, bottled is a combination of tomatoes, onions, peppers, vinegar, herbs and spices.

rice

BASMATI white, fragrant, long-grained rice. It should be washed several times before cooking.

BROWN natural whole grain.

LONG-GRAIN elongated grains.

WILD from North America; not a member of the rice family. It is expensive as it is difficult to cultivate. It has a distinctive flavour.

risoni pasta in the shape of a rice grain.

sake Japan's favourite rice wine; used in cooking, marinating and as part of dipping sauces. If sake is unavailable, dry sherry, vermouth or brandy can be substituted.

sambal oelek (also ulek or olek) a paste made from ground chillies and salt.

satay sauce a spicy sauce made from peanuts, soy sauce, ginger, chilli, onion, garlic, sugar and oil.

scallops we used the scallops with coral (roe) attached.

scampi similar to a prawn but much larger.

sichuan pepper mix also known as chinese pepper; a hot, aromatic combination of pepper, garlic, sugar and onion.

silverbeet also known as swiss chard and (incorrectly) spinach; a member of the beet family, grown for its tasty green leaves and celery-like stems. Best cooked rather than eaten raw.

snow peas also known as mange tout ("eat all").

snow pea sprouts sprouted seeds of the snow pea.

stock 1 cup (250ml) stock is the equivalent of 1 cup (250ml) water plus 1 crumbled stock cube (or 1 teaspoon stock powder).

sugar, brown a soft, fine granulated sugar containing molasses.

sugar snap peas small pods with small, formed peas inside; they are eaten whole, cooked or uncooked.

tabasco sauce made with vinegar, hot red peppers and salt.

teriyaki sauce based on the lighter Japanese soy sauce; contains sugar, spices and vinegar.

tofu also known as bean curd. Firm, soft and silken textures are available.

tomatoes

PASTE a concentrated tomato puree.

PUREE canned, pureed tomatoes. Use fresh, peeled, pureed tomatoes as a substitute, if preferred.

SAUCE tomato ketchup.

SUN-DRIED we use dried tomatoes bottled in oil, unless otherwise specified.

tomato pasta sauce bottled prepared sauce available from supermarkets.

watercress member of the mustard family; small round leaves with a peppery flavour.

zucchini also known as courgette; green, yellow or grey member of the squash family having edible flowers.

soba noodles · *rice vermicelli* · *thick egg noodles* · *instant noodles* · *rice-stick noodles* · *cellophane noodles* · *hokkien noodles* · *fresh rice noodles* · *thin egg noodles*

index

facts and figures

Wherever you live, you'll be able to use our recipes with the help of these easy-to-follow conversions. While these conversions are approximate only, the difference between an exact and the approximate conversion of various liquid and dry measures is but minimal and will not affect your cooking results.

dry measures

metric	imperial
15g	1/2oz
30g	1oz
60g	2oz
90g	3oz
125g	4oz (1/4lb)
155g	5oz
185g	6oz
220g	7oz
250g	8oz (1/2lb)
280g	9oz
315g	10oz
345g	11oz
375g	12oz (3/4lb)
410g	13oz
440g	14oz
470g	15oz
500g	16oz (1lb)
750g	24oz (1 1/2lb)
1kg	32oz (2lb)

liquid measures

metric	imperial
30ml	1 fluid oz
60ml	2 fluid oz
100ml	3 fluid oz
125ml	4 fluid oz
150ml	5 fluid oz (1/4 pint/1 gill)
190ml	6 fluid oz
250ml	8 fluid oz
300ml	10 fluid oz (1/2 pint)
500ml	16 fluid oz
600ml	20 fluid oz (1 pint)
1000ml (1 litre)	1 3/4 pints

helpful measures

metric	imperial
3mm	1/8in
6mm	1/4in
1cm	1/2in
2cm	3/4in
2.5cm	1in
5cm	2in
6cm	2 1/2in
8cm	3in
10cm	4in
13cm	5in
15cm	6in
18cm	7in
20cm	8in
23cm	9in
25cm	10in
28cm	11in
30cm	12in (1ft)

helpful measures

The difference between one country's measuring cups and another's is, at most, within a 2 or 3 teaspoon variance. (For the record, 1 Australian metric measuring cup holds approximately 250ml.) The most accurate way of measuring dry ingredients is to weigh them. When measuring liquids, use a clear glass or plastic jug with the metric markings. (One Australian metric tablespoon holds 20ml; one Australian metric teaspoon holds 5ml.)

If you would like to purchase *The Australian Women's Weekly* Test Kitchen's metric measuring cups and spoons (as approved by Standards Australia), turn to page 120 for details and order coupon. You will receive:

- a graduated set of 4 cups for measuring dry ingredients, with sizes marked on the cups.
- a graduated set of 4 spoons for measuring dry and liquid ingredients, with amounts marked on the spoons.

Note: North America, NZ and the UK use 15ml tablespoons. All cup and spoon measurements are level.

We use large eggs having an average weight of 60g.

oven temperatures

These oven temperatures are only a guide. Always check the manufacturer's manual.

	°C (Celsius)	°F (Fahrenheit)	Gas Mark
Very slow	120	250	1
Slow	150	300	2
Moderately slow	160	325	3
Moderate	180 - 190	350 - 375	4
Moderately hot	200 - 210	400 - 425	5
Hot	220 - 230	450 - 475	6
Very hot	240 - 250	500 - 525	7

how to measure

When using graduated metric measuring cups, shake dry ingredients loosely into the appropriate cup. Do not tap the cup on a bench or tightly pack the ingredients unless directed to do so. Level top of measuring cups and measuring spoons with a knife. When measuring liquids, place a clear glass or plastic jug with metric markings on a flat surface to check accuracy at eye level.

Looking after your interest...

Keep your ACP cookbooks clean, tidy and within easy reach with slipcovers designed to hold up to 12 books. *Plus* you can follow our recipes perfectly with a set of accurate measuring cups and spoons, as used by *The Australian Women's Weekly* Test Kitchen.

TO ORDER

Mail or fax Photocopy and complete the coupon below and post to ACP Books Reader Offer, ACP Publishing, GPO Box 4967, Sydney NSW 2001, *or* fax to (02) 9267 4967.

Phone Have your credit card details ready, then phone 136 116 (Mon-Fri, 8.00am-6.00pm; Sat, 8.00am-6.00pm).

PRICE

Book Holder
Australia: $13.10 (incl. GST).
Elsewhere: $A21.95.

Metric Measuring Set
Australia: $6.50 (incl. GST).
New Zealand: $8.00.
Elsewhere: $A9.95.
Prices include postage and handling.
This offer is available in all countries.

PAYMENT

Australian residents We accept the credit cards listed on the coupon, money orders and cheques.
Overseas residents We accept the credit cards listed on the coupon, drafts in $A drawn on an Australian bank, and also British, New Zealand and U.S. cheques in the currency of the country of issue. Credit card charges are at the exchange rate current at the time of payment.

- -

☐ BOOK HOLDER   ☐ METRIC MEASURING SET

Please indicate number(s) required.

Mr/Mrs/Ms _____

Address _____

_____

Postcode _____ Country _____

Ph: Bus. Hours:( )_____

I enclose my cheque/money order for $ _____ payable to ACP Publishing

OR: please charge my

☐ Bankcard ☐ Visa ☐ MasterCard ☐ Diners Club ☐ Amex

☐☐☐☐☐☐☐☐☐☐☐☐☐☐☐☐☐☐

Expiry Date ____/____

Cardholder's signature _____

Please allow up to 30 days for delivery within Australia. Allow up to 6 weeks for overseas deliveries. Both offers expire 31/12/02.
HLSS02